Brian

THE BOOK OF TORBAY

• A CENTURY OF CELEBRATION •

Frank Pearce

HALSGROVE

First published in Great Britain in 1999

Copyright © 1999 Frank Pearce

*All rights reserved. No part of this publication may be reproduced,
stored in a retrieval system, or transmitted in any form or by any means
without the prior permission of the copyright holder.*

British Library Cataloguing-in-Publication Data
A CIP record for this title is available from the British Library

ISBN 1 84114-029-5

HALSGROVE
PUBLISHING, MEDIA AND DISTRIBUTION

Halsgrove House
Lower Moor Way
Tiverton, Devon EX16 6SS
Tel: 01884 243242
Fax: 01884 243325
email www.halsgrove.com

DEDICATION

To Joan
for her support and
nostalgic contributions

and

To Chris and Linda who
persuaded me to write this book

Printed and bound in Great Britain by Bookcraft Ltd, Midsomer Norton

Contents

Foreword	5
1 – A Place Fit for Kings	7
2 – Bathing and the Marine Spa	11
3 – Murder at Babbacombe	23
4 – Anstey's Cove and Paignton Pier	25
5 – Torre Abbey	27
6 – Oldway Mansion and the Singer Family	29
7 – Harbourside Life, Brixham	31
8 – From Village to Town	33
9 – By the Seaside	39
10 – Transport of Delight	41
11 – High Days and Holidays	49
12 – The Home Fleet in Torbay	57
13 – Flights of Fancy	63
14 – Paignton - In on the Act	65
15 – Dellers Café	67
16 – Cinema Entertainment in Torbay	69
17 – Torquay's Famous Pavilion	71
18 – Torbay in the Great War	75
19 – Into the Roaring Twenties	83
20 – The Thirties and Beyond	87
21 – The Torquay Flood	93
22 – Paignton's Church Street Fair, 1941	95
23 – The Clouds of War	97
24 – Torbay's Home Front	101
25 – Bombs Over the Bay	105
26 – The Yanks are Coming	109
27 – Celebrations	113
28 – Picture Parade	118
Subscribers	125

The Grand Hotel and Torquay Road, c.1920.

Oft in the stilly night,
Ere slumber's chain has bound us,
Fond memory brings the light,
Of other days around us;
The smiles the tears,
of Childhood years;
The words of love then spoken.

Foreword

As its title obviously implies, this book is about Torbay, about its three towns of Torquay, Paignton and Brixham, encapsulated in this blue and silver gulf of sea which has enchanted generations of residents and visitors alike over many years. Having lived, dwelt and had my being in all three places for over half a century, I feel no-one can deny my claim to write about this golden enclave and share with me the affection we all feel for our Torbay.

In the last 150 years it has grown from a simple watering place into a sophisticated holiday resort of the highest standard. Over that period, the rich the poor, the noble and the ignoble, the famous and the infamous have all rendered their salutations to this Golden Crescent. This book mainly covers the period from the mid 1850s up to the mid 1900s, this being the time during which the resort towns underwent their greatest changes.

The book is as much about Torbay's people as its places; how they fared through two World Wars, through bad times and good and how, despite the setbacks, they managed to maintain Torbay's tradition as the acknowledged English Riviera.

Many friends and acquaintances have been most kind and helpful in encouraging the publication of this book and I can only hope that the finished publication will reward their confidence in my efforts to faithfully recall 'past times'. Particular thanks are due to the following organisations and individuals for photographs and other material: Brixham Museum; Mrs Brimicombe; Derek Cox; Judy Diss; Max Danby of Flair Photography; Jackie Fauset formerly of the Imperial Hotel; Mr T. Fromm, General Manager of the Imperial Hotel; Elsie Lamacraft; David Mason; Ray Nickells; Peggy Parnell; Violet Powell; John Pike; Derek Pearce; Mark Poole of the Torquay Library; Mrs B. Sutton; Mike Thompson of the *Herald & Express* for his considerable support and contributions; Mrs P. Tully; Gerald Wasley; Edna White; Phylis White and Keith Williams.

Frank Pearce
Torbay, 1999

A view across Torquay harbour, 1842.

1 – A Place Fit for Kings

This book cannot, and does not claim, to cover every aspect of local history from the early days, but research has retrieved some fleeting images of the past and here presents them with affection and sincerity.

As the joyous bells rang out at midnight at the window of the twentieth century, the wind of change was already blowing, heralding the birth of a new era that would effect every village, town and city throughout Great Britain. Prior to this, the late 1800s had been spent in a sunset of comparative calm. When in January 1901, Queen Victoria , who had reigned with constancy and probity for sixty-four years, died in her eighty-second year, she left a succession of three future kings ; the philandering Edward VII, the impassive George V, and the enigmatic and unpredictable Edward VIII who was to abdicate after a few months.

The early years of the new century ushered in a period of social unrest and global turbulence; the Boer war in South Africa 1899, the early signals of revolution in Russia 1905, and disaster at sea with the sinking of the supposedly unsinkable liner *Titanic* in 1912. There came also women's militant demands for the right to vote; the birth of the Suffragette movement in 1903 leading to disobedience and violence and later, with the emergence of Trade Unionism, frequent strikes. Socially, class distinction was glaringly evident with the population divided into two categories, the rich and the poor.

Large houses in towns and cities and particularly in Torquay were occupied by the wealthy who maintained an army of domestic servants to subscribe to their every comfort. In the mid 1860s it was the custom of the 'well-to-do' to come to Torquay and hire large detached villas, complete

This must be one of the earliest photographs of a family group in Torquay. Dated 1865, it reveals how, by mid-Victorian times, there was a desire to be seen to be improving oneself, through dress and social manners.

with servant's halls and people to fill them. As late as 1871, there were 12 772 females in Torquay to 8885 males and, allowing for a few hundred widows and elderly spinsters amongst the 3000 householders, it is clear there was a veritable army of women in domestic service.

Some of these desirable dwellings were sited in the Higher Lincombes and Higher Warberrys giving commanding panoramic views of the whole of Torbay. In the light of present-day working conditions, the term 'servant' of those pre- and past Victorian days might be more truly described as 'serf' for the wage for a sixteen-hour-day was rewarded with the princely sum of around £20 per year.

In the ordinary elementary schools, education for children of the working class was basic and often harsh. Bitterly cold class rooms holding around sixty children were the order of the day. In some cases, education was delivered and controlled by an eagle-eyed master who ruled by wielding his cane like a whirling sabre. The penalty for not knowing the answer to a question was either a caning, a clip across the ear or a sound cuff to the head. It was, in effect, education by fear. Consequently, for the backward boys in particular, school was looked upon with dread, a place overshadowed by a reign of terror.

The literature of Victorian fiction, often portrayed two opposing viewpoints of life in the mid 1800s. The presentation of 'Merry England', of red faced squires, laughing buxom maidens, rose covered cottages and plum puddings caricatured on Christmas cards, was largely a figment of sentimental imagination. The enchanting popular fiction of those days flowed more readily from the pens of Trollope and Thackeray than that of Dickens who was far more willing to reveal the squalor, hardships and conditions of the working classes than those of the elegant lifestyle of the gentry.

Torbay's place as one of Britain's premier holiday resorts has its roots in the Victorian's passion for bathing. But as a natural harbour, the place was long before known to sailors as a safe haven, and the bay has witnessed many historic maritime events. The Armada passed close to Berry Head in 1588, and William of Orange, future king, chose Brixham as the landing point for his 15 000-strong invading army. The Emperor Napoleon was brought to Torbay aboard the *Bellerephon* on his way into exile, here to parade haughtily on deck while visitors flocked just to get a glimpse. In September 1855, Napoleon's nephew came voluntarily to visit the town, and in the following year the floating gun

Precursor to the famous Imperial, Webb's Royal Hotel, seen here c. 1850, was one of the Victorian resort's most fashionable hotels.

Signature of Louis-Napoleon III, ex-Emperor of France.

battery *Dragon*, belonging to Napoleon III, anchored in the bay for several days.

Torquay's initial development as a resort was mainly due to the aspirations and spirited enthusiasm of Sir Lawrence Palk, Bart, MP who had a dream that one day the town would possess the best hotel in Devon. Much to his pleasure and satisfaction that dream was to become a reality for now, elegantly poised on high land close to the rise of Beacon Hill and with breathtaking views of Torbay, stands the 154 bedroomed hotel, the Imperial. It has an intrinsic and hereditary affiliation with the history of the resort; originally on that site in 1852 stood a dwelling known as Webb's Royal Hotel.

In 1863, under the direction of Palk, the Torquay Hotel Company was formed and a new lease of the site was granted by him for a tenure of 99 years; the ground rent amounting to only £60 per annum. The purpose of the new company was to acquire the existing Webb's Hotel and to build a new, larger hotel to be the biggest and best in the area. Although the foundation stone was laid in March 1864, the Imperial was not declared open until 3 November 1866, with Mr Thomas Webb of the former Royal Hotel installed as Manager. Success was instantaneous, its fame spreading far and wide. Since its inauguration its regal title has been amply justified by the high standard of comfort, care and cuisine the hotel provides.

From then to the present day, that criteria of excellence has been patronised and enjoyed by many English and Continental Royal families. For instance Napoleon III spent some of his exile here, for on 11 September 1871, we read that:

> 'the ex-Emperor Napoleon III, with the Prince Imperial arrived in Torquay and took up his residence at the Imperial Hotel, where he remained for five weeks. On the 4 October, he honoured the Torquay Rowing Club by accepting an invitation to take a cruise on the water.'

The date of Napoleon III's journey to Torquay by rail was seemingly well-known, and to avoid a crush, Torquay station was cordoned off with only a limited number of persons admitted. However, the station yard, Torbay Road and roads leading to the Imperial were lined with people.

In February 1870, the Queen of Holland with her entire entourage stayed here for some time. The surviving visitors' book records in perfect copperplate handwriting the testimony of her arrival: 'Sa Majesté la Reine des Pays Bas'. Queen Sophie was the first wife of William III, King of the Netherlands who reigned from 1869 to 1890.

During the late 1800s, the hotel was greatly extended to accommodate many more distinguished visitors, among whom were Prince Esterhazy of Hungary, Adalbert Prince of Prussia, the Princes John and Francis Liechtenstein of Austria, Alexandrea Baschmakow, Master of the Court of His imperial Majesty Emperor of Russia, St Petersburg, and many more.

In October 1877, the Prince of Wales, the future King Edward VII, with his two sons, Albert Victor and George (later King George V), spent some time at the Imperial and later enjoyed trips up the River Dart to Totnes and Berry Pomeroy.

King Edward VII, a celebrated visitor to Torbay as the Prince of Wales in 1877.

The Marine Spa and Beacon Cove, Torquay c. 1960.

The Marine Spa Swimming Bath which functioned from 1913 to 1971.

2 – Bathing and the Marine Spa

In the mid 1800s, there evolved a cult, convinced that sea-water was a near infallible cure for almost every disorder, and a magical tonic for the lungs, stomach and blood cells. With this belief firmly entrenched more and more people came to the seaside. Where better than the safe and warm beaches of Torbay?

Then someone hit on the idea of a warm water indoor swimming bath in Torquay and, in 1817, a certain Dr Pollard built a bath of sorts on the site of what is now the Regina Hotel at the bottom of Beacon Hill. By 1892, the requirements of the Torbay area had outgrown the capabilities of the Bath House, and in that year, a company was formed to build an open air bath on the seaward side of the rocks below Beacon Hill. The scheme involved the flattening of the front of the promontory and by 1898 provided a flood bath exposed to the sea as part of the whole building known as the Bath's Saloon and which were declared open at a special gala.

The bath was 45 feet square, open to the sea at one end through four wide arches but, subject to tide and storm, the bath was never a success and later abandoned. The project lost money and the shareholders, who sold the building for £3500, had to find £13 000 out of their own pockets.

Later William Kitson bought the building and flattened the rest of the promontory to build Haldon Pier on behalf of the Haldon Estates. Above the promontory he also built a great room to provide a skating rink. However, sixteen years later, the building was occupied by the Local Board, forerunner of the Corporation. Then, in 1897, a meeting was held by the swimming fraternity at Haarer's Restaurant next to the old Burlington Cinema, near the Post Office in Fleet Street. Here the new Torquay Leander Swimming and Life Saving Society was formed whose members were to bring considerable honours to the town in the world of National and International Swimming events.

Among its founder members, the names of Bill Luscombe, 'Tack' Collings, Sydney Coombes, Charles Downey and Thomas Bond emerge; men who not only effectively subscribed to but active-

Torquay Leander Xmas dip, 1900.

ly launched the Society on its successful career. It must be said however, that these five were the nucleus of members, known as the Torquay Swimming Club which existed long before the Society was formed and many years prior to the building of the famed Marine Spa.

FUTURE OLYMPIC STAR

The Society at this point in its history was specialising in its divers and, with three excellent boards from which to train the members, began to be highly proficient in the art. Little wonder, for none other than Torquay's future Olympic star was giving them the necessary coaching: 'Tack' Collings at this time was one of the finest trick divers in Great Britain. He went annually to the National Championships at Highgate Ponds in London to participate.

Those were the days when the world-renowned Swedish diver Haljmar Johannsen carried all before him, but as a high diver 'Tack' stood alone in the West. A few years later he represented Britain in the 1908 Olympic Games in London.

And so from early beginnings, honours were created for Torquay. In 1906 W.J. Luscombe (Bill) of the Torquay *Herald Express* took over as general secretary of the Society from Mr York Wood.

Under their new title, the official removal to Peaked Tor in 1900 was an historic affair. The opening dip and rally was attended by 100 swimmers, together with hundreds of spectators who lined the slopes. After the usual photographs and the mass plunge there came the great event. It

In 1900 'Tack' Collings performed his famous dive from the 60 feet Saddle Rock at Peaked Tor into only 9 feet of water.

was billed as 'The Sensation of the Day' and no better event could have been staged. It was a dive by Leander founder member 'Tack' Collings who did a remarkable and dangerous double somersault dive from Saddle Rock, sixty feet above high water-mark, into only nine feet of water.

Long distance swimming was also a popular feature in those days and occasionally, when the fleet was in the bay, some of the more ambitious members would swim out to the nearest warship anchored a mile or more off Saddle Rock. More than once, a nip of rum was offered by the Royal Navy lads and gladly accepted.

When the Olympic Games trials were held in 1928 at Blackpool, Leander had no less than six representatives, three women and three men. Competition was extremely keen and there were doubts whether the West would secure representation at the Games in Paris. But to everyone's

Many Torquinians will remember Mr W. J. Luscombe of the Herald Express. *He was a familiar figure in the towns of Torbay.*

THE BOOK OF TORBAY

Leander Xmas dip, Peaked Tor, 1906.

delight, the youngest in the party, Glady's Luscombe, a schoolgirl at Torquay Girl's Grammar School, was selected. Thus Torquay secured its second and youngest international star.

The Marine Spa Swimming bath and Medical Baths were started in 1913, but work was delayed due to the First World War and not completed until 1915, the whole project costing between £17 000 and £20 000. The heated salt water bath was partly glass covered and measured 90 feet by 30 feet, a good size for those days, and which in its time has produced some outstanding swimmers and divers of Olympic standard.

At that time there was little, if any, teaching of the art of swimming in the town. The youngsters simply had to do the best they could and teach one another under the most primitive conditions. The swimming activities of Leander from the 1850's had to be confined to the nearby small beach of Peaked Tor below the Imperial Hotel for the men, and to Beacon Cove for the ladies. Mixed bathing was 'taboo', for it was considered quite improper for men to even watch ladies bathing. What their roving eyes might have seen is a mystery, for the girls were completely enveloped in voluminous costumes covering them from neckline to ankle.

For the men however it was a different matter for they had Peaked Tor where the few events of those days took place. In the indoor swimming bath the water depth was increased from 4 feet 6 inches at the shallow end to 7 feet 6 inches at the deep end where three diving boards were provided. Upstairs, a balcony which overlooked the whole length and width of the pool accommodated several public bathrooms, and provided spectator facilities for the enjoyment of those who later came to watch the highly competitive galas.

In 1921, Leander were in financial difficulties and decided to hold a dance. The only place large enough to accommodate the numbers envisaged was the then Marine Spa indoor skating rink (later the Spa Ballroom). At that time this part of the Spa had only been used as a skating rink. Having hired the place for the occasion, the swimming committee rolled up their sleeves and scrubbed

Band rehearsal in the Marine Spa Ballroom, 1920s.

the whole floor of this great room. They then followed up the effort by using sandstone bricks to smooth down the rough surface and finished the job with a rotating polisher. The dance that followed was such a financial success and proved so popular that the council decided to adopt the same idea and then promoted their own dances. It was from the efforts of Leander that the old skating rink was then converted into the Marine Spa Ballroom.

It was a beautiful room where, as time passed, dance entertainment grew more and more popular, with thousands coming from all parts for its tea dances and evening dances. Here, couples swayed to the rhythm and music of the famous bands of Victor Sylvester, Henry Hall, Ted Heath, Ivy Benson's All Women's Band and so on. These were great occasions and many a romance that blossomed from the Spa Ballroom music led to the chimes of church wedding bells.

During the period 1913 to 1922, the building had been developed to include medical baths, and these were further extended from 1922 to cover more treatments. These included seaweed baths, mud baths, peat baths, vapour, brine, and needle baths. Altogether, a total of forty different treatments were available. There was also a luxurious cooling lounge where patients could rest after their medical applications. This was a spacious, room containing luxury seating, its walls and ceilings embellished with rich gilt moulding reliefs. Gracious comfort indeed, akin to a palace. By 1929, the lovely Vita-glass sun lounge was extended to 90 feet, making it the largest in Britain. At the seaward end was a large stillroom where catering was prepared for the morning, afternoon and evening customers.

It can be claimed that over its one hundred years existence, Leander, along with the neighbouring Oddicombe S.C., has made an important contribution to the safety and physical welfare of the town's residents. From the intensive programme of instruction by the skilled few, many thousands were taught to swim and to enjoy the benefits of this health giving sport.

To provide a sense of privacy to the ladies at Beacon Cove, bushes trees and a high fence were

The Vita-glass sun lounge at the Marina Spa, 1930s.

established on the higher ground to shut out the gaze of inquisitive males. On seats just above the cove were notices to the effect they were not to be occupied by males during the hours of bathing. In fact, a man called Bill Ford was employed by the Council as a guard to physically stop men from looking down on the ladies bathing!

On 2 September 1930, a serious accident occurred in the Spa swimming bath that brought National headlines. It was in fact the most astounding accident in swimming bath history. A girl swimmer was sucked through the outlet pipe into the sea. To everyone's astonishment she survived the terrible ordeal.

The event occurred at lunchtime when the bath had been cleared of the few swimmers who were there, to allow it to be emptied. There was a circular vent in the bottom of the wall at the deep end barely 12 inches in diameter, leading to a similar size pipe which emptied into the sea at Beacon Cove. The attendant, having checked that the bath was clear, opened the outlet valve to empty it. Unknown to him, a young girl swimmer was talking to a friend on the top diving board and, unaware that the bath was emptying, took a dive which brought her feet in line with the outlet pipe.

The enormous suction produced by 90 000 gallons of water pouring through such a small aperture, sucked the girl in and on through 100 feet of iron pipe, depositing her into some four feet of sea water.

Although she was terribly lacerated from the rusty barnacles in the pipe, she staggered a few yards up the beach before collapsing. Press publicity was kept to a minimum but this sort of news could not be entirely suppressed, and the story went all over the world.

Whether the accident influenced the council no one knows, but some time later, when the swimming bath was redeveloped, the vent was replaced by a smaller aperture in the bath floor at the deep end through which the water was slowly processed into a filtration system. With this done it was assumed that a similar accident could never happen again.

At most of the Spa galas there was much friendly rivalry between the two clubs of Leander and Oddicombe. Each race was keenly contested especially in the team events when the races produced so much enthusiasm from spectators that the cheers could be heard at the bottom of Beacon Hill.

THE BOOK OF TORBAY

Beacon Cove c.1933, showing, on the left, the walls of the Marine Spa swimming bath. This is the location where the young girl was ejected into the sea after being sucked through the pool outlet. A section of the pipe shows as a dark shadow running down the beach towards the water's edge. Miraculously the girl survived and lived to old age. Above the walls of the swimming bath, extreme left, can be seen the windows of the Vita-glass sun lounge.

A NEW CHAMPION

It was in 1931 that Monica Pearce, a young up-and-coming swimmer and diver won her first County Championship and during the next twenty years she became one of Torquay's leading sporting personalities, and winner of over 30 Western and Devon County championships in swimming and diving. During those years she created a county record by winning the highboard diving championship seven times. In addition to Western and Devon County championships, Monica competed on several occasions in the National Diving Championships at Blackpool, Jersey and New Brighton, and was twice runner-up in the Nationals, on one occasion missing the title by one point. She was also Britain's reserve for the Olympic Games in 1936.

WATER BALLET

In the spring of 1948, Leander Committee members decided to introduce swimming entertain-

Leander's national champion diver, Monica Pearce.

Monica Pearce of Torquay Leander competing in the National Diving Championships at Blackpool in 1936. She also represented Great Britain and Torquay at the 1936 Olympics in Munich.

ment in the form of synchronised swimming to music by a team of girl swimmers. This was an entirely new approach and Leander was probably the first club in Britain to introduce successful 'Water Ballet' as it came to be called.

Such was the show's popularity, it was little realised that the club had committed itself to putting on the Water Ballet, every fortnight, through each summer for the next twelve years. That period between 1948 and 1960 was a very busy time for the club, for championship successes went hand in hand with Water Ballet presentations.

ZENITH OF POPULARITY

It is fair to say that those years represented the very peak of the Marine Spa's notability as a place of summer entertainment. It was quite a common sight on those occasions to see a queue of people stretching from the swimming bath entrance, up the steps, along the car park and part way down Beacon Hill. Capacity houses were the order of the day, often many were turned away, and on occasions the ballet presentations were made into civic receptions. Coachloads of spectators arrived from Dorset,

Oddicombe Swimming Club, 1926. The picture includes Mr Hield (Torquay Town Clerk); Mrs Hield; Col. Rowland Ward; Henry Thomas; Messrs Moon, Cox, Hider, Atkins, Kent, Bowden, Bicknell, Causley, Byle, Brown, Banks, Clow, and Reg French (top right), for many years Club Secretary.

THE BOOK OF TORBAY

Left: *Leander's First Water Ballet team posing for the photographer after one of their displays 'The Water Lily' scene. They are: Audrey Baigent; Yvonne Schroder; Jean Bullock; Jean Hern; Pauline Hayward; Margaret Short; Geraldine Vinnicombe; Glennis Phillips, Doris Bond; Kathleen Bond; Ann Margetts; Stella Margetts; Monica Pearce; Shirley Cann; Vanessa Marchant.*

Right: *Leander's lady swimmers with their presentation of old-fashioned bathing costumes at the Marine Spa sun lounge in 1948.*

Left: *Leander's young swimming champions of 1955, representing Torquay in the English Schools Championships. (l-r): Tony Rees; Nigel Salsbury; Maurice Martin; Joan Hewitt; Ann Newcombe; Irene Nicholls; John Holding; Ivor Bartlett.*

Right: *The Leander Opening Dip at Beacon Cove in May, 1969. Mrs Stella Margetts being presented with a silver tray by the Chairman Frank Pearce, for her many years of service to the club as Competition Secretary. Behind Mrs Margetts is Mr Eddie Blackler (President) and extreme right Mr Ted Windeatt.*

Somerset, Gloucester, North Devon and Cornwall. In September 1930, among the audience were 250 officials of the Amateur Swimming Association, the President of the A.S.A., and the civic heads of Torquay, Paignton, Dartmouth, Brixham and Newton Abbot.

MANY YOUNG PEOPLE.

With so many young people at the Spa Swimming Bath on club nights, it was inevitable that friendships should blossom into courtship and eventual marriage. The realisation of the passing of the years came when these young married couples brought their children along to the Spa to be taught to swim and when these children grew up, married and brought their children along. At one time there were four generations of one family in the club.

A CORNERSTONE

Throughout the major part of the life of Torquay Leander there had been one person who became a cornerstone in the history of swimming activities – the late Mrs Stella Margetts. She joined the committee in 1930 and became the Devon County Ladies Freestyle champion in 1931. For 18 years she held the post of Devon County Competition Secretary and, following this, recognition of her dedication to swimming came thick and fast. She became President of Devon County in 1958, President of the West in 1972, and President of Leander in 1973. But the crowning achievement came when she was appointed President of the Amateur Swimming Association of Great Britain and inducted into that office at the Annual General Meeting and Banquet held at the Grand Hotel in Torquay in 1984. A great occasion indeed and one of which the club is justifiably proud. There is no doubt that it was her organising ability, her inspiration, and personality that kept Leander to the forefront of continuing success.

The names already mentioned in this account are of course only part of a long list who have given great and valuable service to thousands of people in Torbay in this medium. The expert knowledge and experience gained by Leander trainees has not been lost however, for many have left these shores to settle in lands overseas, and there to establish swimming clubs. It is exemplified in the case of Christine Pain, a former Leander and Devon County Champion who with her husband, Dr David Margetts, settled in Canada. At Elliott Lake she is a founder member of two successful Aquatic clubs, is chairman for the Canadian Amateur Swimming Association and head of the coaching committee for the North Eastern Ontario Sports Council.

A CHAMPION FOR DEVON

In the early 1960s there emerged from the trainees a young boy who was to make swimming history. His name, Malcolm Windeatt, who at that time was to become not only the greatest swimmer in the county of Devon but the fastest swimmer in Great Britain; winning over 67 County titles. From 1963 to 1970 he won seven National championships and had the distinction of representing Torquay in the Commonwealth Games at Edinburgh.

Malcolm Windeatt in 1972, was selected to swim for Great Britain at the Olympic Games in Munich.

Stella Margetts with her swimming trophies.

THE BOOK OF TORBAY

Torquay Leander's Christmas dip at Beacon Cove in 1954. The crowded terraces reveal just how well these occasions were attended.

BBC commentator, Johnny Morris, interviewing swimmer, Pat Whittaker, at the Leander Christmas dip in 1951.

The schoolroom at St Vincent's Orphanage, at which school the boy who died in the swimming pool tragedy was a pupil.

A TRAGEDY

It was in 1963 that the first rumblings of disquiet were heard when council officials began to voice their misgivings about the condition of the Marine Spa Swimming Bath. In a report dated January 1964, the then Local Medical Officer of Health Dr K. MacTaggart, stated that there were many aspects in which the bath fell short of standards of health, safety and convenience. A few years later, following an inspection by Torbay's Chief Architect, Mr Banks, it was also found that the foundations and lower walls were giving cause for concern and three large steel girders had to be positioned across the width of the bath to support the outer wall which was gradually moving inward. Additionally other signs of decay and general deterioration were plainly visible. As a result, expert opinion came to the reluctant conclusion that the bath could not be saved; it was dangerous and would have to be demolished.

The council were not quite sure when, but in July 1971, the decision was made for them by the ghastly tragedy of an 11-year-old boy from St Vincent's Orphanage, Torquay who was sucked through the narrow filtration pipe in the bottom of the bath; an accident which seemed virtually impossible. As a result, an army of workmen toiled ceaselessly for 26 hours to reach the body wedged 10 feet up inside the pipe.

The disaster spelt the end of the Marine Spa Swimming Bath and, as a consequence of Torquay Leander's HQ. On the 27 September 1971, the bulldozers began demolition. Sadly, this was

The Marine Spa Ballroom during its demolition in 1971.

immediately followed by the dismantling of the rest of the Spa; the Ballroom, the Medical baths, the Vita-glass sun lounge and everything else.

It was not only the end of the Marine Spa but the end of an era, especially for the historic ballroom. The walls and ceilings which had echoed to the excitement, the applause and the music of famous bands, to whispered romances, jealousies and joys, are now but a memory.

THE FUTURE

As far as Torbay swimmers were concerned the demolition of the Spa swimming bath was a crushing blow for it left the borough without a covered pool. Naturally, this state of affairs produced a storm of protest but Torquay Town Council in the meantime were busily developing plans for a super pool at Clennon Valley.

While this in the long term would no doubt prove satisfactory, the Torquay Leander and Oddicombe Swimming Club committees, impatient at the constant delays and indecisions, presented an application to the council for permission to build a pool at Plainmoor.

In late 1971, the Torbay Park's Committee approved a plan in principle and although the project was subjected to further delays and setbacks, eventually, through dogged determination and hard work, the Plainmoor pool was built and opened for training use on 22 August 1977. But that period between the closing of the Spa Bath and the opening of the Plainmoor Pool was a wilderness time when the Society had no home. They were faced with falling membership and few places to hire a little swimming time.

Over its 100 years Leander has been not so much a Society as an institution, so synonymous with Torquay that it became a part and parcel of its history and tradition. Now at Plainmoor there is a new spirit, a new team of dedicated teachers and committee members, a new generation of swimmers, with new' potential champions emerging to follow and emulate the successes of past great swimmers who brought honour and prestige to Torquay in its one hundred historic years.

THE BOOK OF TORBAY

Above: *The Glen, the thatched home of the murdered Miss Emma Keyse.* Inset left: *John Lee.* Inset right: *Miss Keyse as a young woman.* Below: *Babbacombe Beach in 1912. By this time The Glen had been demolished.* Bottom: *Beach Cottage, Babbacombe, 1908.*

3 – Murder at Babbacombe

When Britain took its first few faltering steps into the 20th century, it discovered an uncertain world. The cost of the Boer War in Africa was dipping deeply into the Chancellor's purse; labour unrest and strikes were prevalent and the militant tactics of some of the extreme suffragettes were most troublesome. Great as had been the general progress in the old Queen's reign it had not been without its drawbacks. The feverish struggle after wealth had led to a worship of money; railways and telegraphs had imparted an impatient rush to keep pace with modern life; cheap mechanical production was proving fatal to former excellence of quality; sudden increases in mining and factory buildings were disfiguring the countryside and, most serious of all, Germany was rapidly increasing her navy, imposing a threat to Britain's control of the world's trade routes. The wonders of new science like electricity, the motor car, Marconi's wireless and the aeroplane, had a devastating effect on the dying breed of Victorians who were convinced that all these new fangled ideas would eventually fade away.

But while Britain was absorbed with the National and International issues of the day, the topic of interest for Torquay residents in December 1907 was the announcement of the release from Portland Convict Prison of a man called John Lee (and infamously known to all as John 'Babbacombe' Lee). His release brought memories flooding back for many Torquinians, as twenty-two years earlier, Lee was known far and as 'The man they could not hang.'

Nestling under the cliffs at Babbacombe was a house known as The Glen, occupied by a benevolent elderly lady, Miss Emma Keyse. She was always ready to help those in need but gullible and easily deceived. She employed as a cook a woman named Elizabeth Harris whose half-brother was John Lee, a man with a police record and a history of convictions. Miss Keyse gave him employment in the house in the hope of setting him on his feet and giving him a new start in life.

On the morning of the 16 November 1884, Elizabeth Harris awoke to find the house on fire. She rushed to the nearby Cary Arms to raise the alarm and, when the neighbours and the police arrived, they found the body of Miss Keyse with her throat cut and skull fractured and, lying by the body, a blood-covered hatchet.

There was evidence of paraffin having been used to start the fire and Lee was found with a cut and bandaged arm, but unable to give a satisfactory explanation for his movements. He was arrested and charged with the murder of Miss Keyse.

On 4 February 1885, Mr Justice Manisty passed sentence of death on Lee and the execution was fixed for 23 February at Exeter.

James Berry, the executioner described how he led the hooded Lee on to the scaffold, positioned him on the trapdoor but when he pulled the lever the door failed to drop. He and the warders then stamped on the door but when the lever was again pulled the door remained shut. Lee was taken away and the trapdoor tested yet appeared to work perfectly. A second attempt was made but again the lever failed to open the door, Lee was moved away and further tests carried out. A sack containing material, the same weight as Lee, was then placed on the trapdoor and that responded to the lever most satisfactorily but when the third attempt was made with Lee on the trapdoor the result was the same as on previous occasions. As a result, the Prison Chaplain the Rev John Petkin then instructed that the execution be postponed.

Following the amazing prison drama, the Home Secretary, Sir William Harcourt, commuted the sentence to penal servitude for life. It was later revealed by the prison Chaplain that Lee had previously told the warders he had dreamed 'the drop' would not act. Lee was not released from prison until December 1907, having served almost twenty-three years. The story has echoed down through the century, to be told and retold many times as. Lee himself wrote an autobiography, *The Man They Could Not Hang,* which enjoyed great notoriety.

THE BOOK OF TORBAY

Left: *A view of Anstey's Cove taken from the hilltop around the turn of the century. Note the wooden bathing machines from which ladies would emerge, clad in voluminous costumes, to bathe.*

Right: *Anstey's Cove c.1900. The small hut with the flagpole suggests that teas and refreshments were available. Note the open-fronted boathouse and the bathing machines lined up waiting for customers.*

Left: *A day out for father, mother and daughter at Anstey's Cove, 1908.*

4 – Anstey's Cove and Paignton Pier

Left: *Paignton Pier ablaze in 1919.*

Right: *A busy afternoon on the Victorian promenade at Paignton in the early 1900s. In the background is Dendy's pier which was opened in 1879.*

In 1878, Mr Hyde Dendy, a wealthy barrister, purchased Teignmouth Pier with the intention of having it removed and re-erected at Paignton, but this was found to be impracticable, so his architect Mr G. S. Bridgman designed a similar but longer pier which was built around 1879. After Dendy's death, ownership passed to the Devon Dock & Steamship Co.

Throughout the summer months before the Great War, the magnificent paddle-steamers the *Duke of Devonshire* and *Duchess of Devonshire*, called regularly at Paignton Pier, filled with holidaymakers crossing the bay from Torquay to Brixham.

At noon on Thursday 18 June 1919, the pier caught fire and blazed furiously for the remainder of the day and was still burning the following morning. A concert party 'The Aristocrats' who were performing there lost all their properties; also the stage fittings originally bought from the Bijou Theatre within the Gerston Hotel (also built by Mr Dendy) were destroyed, including the grand piano which crashed into the sea.

In 1940, the army cut away a large section of the pier at the shore end as an anti-invasion measure. They also dug a deep trench in the sand from the Redcliffe Hotel to the Harbour but this was promptly levelled by the next high tide.

A sunny afternoon' stroll along Paignton's promenade in 1905.

Paignton sands 1906, showing the bathing machines which were drawn by horses to the water's edge. They were sometimes taken right into the sea to allow modest lady bathers to emerge and walk down the steps into the water. Mixed bathing was not permitted; and there was a special session allowed for ladies only and another for gentlemen. In the distance on the right can be seen the Paignton Gentlemen's Club, opened in 1885.

5 – Torre Abbey

Torquay has grown up around the site of the original settlement of Torre Abbey. Built in 1196, the monks were forced to abandon the abbey during the reign of Henry VIII, the scourge of the Monasteries. The abbey was bought by the Cary family in 1662, and after the death of the last Cary occupant, in 1929, the local authorities bought the estate.

Dedicated to St Norbert, the abbey was founded by Lord Brewere, one of the most powerful barons of the day. He owned the barony of Tor, among other possessions. He richly endowed the abbey and bestowed it on the monks. In its day it was a magnificent edifice as the ruins today remind us. The bulk of the buildings have been transformed into the present residential mansion.

In the grounds are still to be seen the ivy covered church tower, the arches of which formed the entrance to the chapter house. There are also remnants of the monastery itself, its tower, the refectory and the grange, the last named generally known as the Spanish Barn. It was here in 1588 that the crew of the captured flagship of the Spanish Armada, the *Don Pedro de Valdez*, was imprisoned. Local legend has it that the barn is haunted.

The west front of Torre Abbey. Founded in twelfth century in the reign of Richard I and now in the hands of the local authority, it is one of the area's greatest historical tourist attractions.

Above: *Isaac Singer's Oldway Mansion, built in 1874. This contrasts with the photograph (below)* showing *cottages in nearby Cecil Road, taken at around the same time. The coexistence of great wealth and poverty was something of a hallmark of mid-Victorian times, as writers such as Charles Dickens starkly portrayed.*

6 – Oldway Mansion and the Singer Family

A building of palatial proportions, Oldway is probably the most photographed location in Torbay. It is certainly regarded as a national tourist attraction and arts venue. Originally built in 1874 by Isaac Singer, the sewing-machine millionaire, it was transformed thirty years later by his son Paris Singer as a miniature Versailles.

The triumphal arch is a replica of Versailles's Trianon gateway, while the colonnaded east front is copied from buildings in Paris' *Place de la Concorde*. The grounds were laid out by the French landscape architect Achille Duchene but the showpiece is Paris Singer's magnificent marble staircase, and the painted ceiling, copied from Louis XIV's 17th century staircase at Versailles, destroyed in 1752. But the jewel in the crown is David's vast painting 'The crowning of Josephine by Napoleon', bought by Singer in 1898 to form a spectacular backdrop to the staircase. Sold back to Versailles in 1946 a reproduction of the painting was bought and restored to its original position in 1995.

THE SINGER FAMILY OF OLDWAY MANSION

Senior residents living in Paignton before the Great War could recall the many benefits which this generous family bestowed on the town. These included the building of Paignton Cottage Hospital.

Isaac Singer's eldest son, Sir Mortimer Singer, was well known for his participation in 'J' class yacht racing and his valiant but unsuccessful attempts to beat Sir Thomas Lipton's *Shamrock*. His many gifts to the town included the Church Choir Vestries completed just before the war.

The second son, Washington Singer, lived at Steartfield House and his racehorses were accommodated in the stables opposite the present Palace Hotel. The stretch of grassland now called Preston Sea Front was used to exercise them. The year 1906 saw the completion of Merritts Flats, a housing project developed by Washington Singer, surely several decades ahead of his time. He was the first President of the Paignton Swimming Club and was also a patron of the Rowing Club.

The third son, Paris Eugene Singer, was perhaps the member of the family best known locally

Isaac Singer - inventor of the sewing machine.

because of his long residence at Oldway and his many activities in Paignton. He undertook the vast scheme of additions and alterations to the Mansion over three years, involving both local and international craftsmen. These renovations were completed in 1907. Paris Eugene also built the Preston sea wall, cut what is now Seaway Road under the bridge, and built an aeroplane hangar against the wall of the Redcliffe Hotel, although the outbreak of the Great War prevented its being used.

Paris Singer gave the organ to the Parish Church and many other generous gifts but his greatest bequest, and a lasting tribute to his memory, was the wish expressed before his death, in June 1932, that the town of Paignton should be given the first opportunity to acquire Oldway at a modest price.

Preston road names are closely linked with the family in Paris Road, Eugene Road, Mortimer Avenue, Cecil Avenue and Laura Grove. In October 1927, the Rotary Club of Paignton accepted two new members on the same day: one was Cecil Singer (whose two young daughters Winnie and Susie inspired the road name Winsu Avenue), the other was John Sutton of the Sutton printing family.

Brixham – from a print made in 1825.

Sailing ships of 1912 in Brixham harbour. The harbour itself had been rebuilt in 1837.

7 – Harbourside Life, Brixham

The harbours of all three Torbay towns have long histories, whether through fishing or trading. Brixham became famous during the nineteenth century for its dark-red sailed trawlers. In 1850 there were 270 trawlers fishing out of Brixham providing work for 1600 seamen as well as work for those at the ports involved in curing and salting herring and pilchards. The industry went into decline due to depletion of the fish stocks and competition from the North Sea fleets based at the East coast ports.

The pictures shown here were taken before the technology of the combustion engine had its impact on the sailing fleet.

Red sailed fishing smacks at rest in Brixham inner harbour in 1897.

The lighthouse at Berry Head, Brixham, in 1906. The Royal Navy sailor's uniform provides an indication of the date.

BRIXHAM HARBOUR

A large two-masted schooner secured alongside the jetty in Brixham harbour, 1912.

Brixham fishing fleet, seen here safely sheltered behind the breakwater, c. 1900.

8 – From Village to Town

This is purported to be the earliest photograph taken of the Old Forge at Cockington, in 1860. It reveals something of the rural atmosphere of South Devon at that time, a place only beginning to be touched by the coming revolution in transport. Cockington was to be joined with Torquay in 1900, although it did not officially become part of the borough until 1928.

Another view of the old forge at Cockington, showing the blacksmith at work.

Like Topsy, Torbay grew gracefully and elegantly; emerging from a period of awakening puberty to the adulthood of a reformation. At the turn of the century it found itself in a turmoil of vacillation, eager to maintain its place in the rapidly moving present, yet desperately clinging to the nostalgic image of its past. The reluctance to change was challenged by the logical conclusion that the alternative was obsolescence. The resort was at a crossroads. Should it exchange its peaceful and tranquil existence for the noise and mayhem of a vigorous and enterprising future?

But the choice was literally taken out of its hands by force of circumstances. The availability of rail travel to those living in the industrial areas of England, Scotland, Wales and London brought Torbay to the top of the holiday resort league. The splendour of its scenery, the remedial advantage of its warm climate and the panoramic beauty of its huge bay brought thousands flocking.

To the working population in the mid-shires, new horizons were appearing; there were new opportunities to be grasped, new pleasures to be enjoyed. Among these, the exciting experience of a holiday by the sea, something hitherto denied to many. And where better than Torbay? For it was no longer just a watering place, somewhere along the south coast; it was *the* place to go for the best of holidays.

Gradually it became known that the three towns of Torquay, Paignton and Brixham catered for most tastes and interests. Soon it attained the

The photographs on these pages remind us of the transformation of Torbay as the area grew into one of the country's premier holiday resorts, and a place for the fashionable to be seen at during the season. Opposite page top: *An 1895 view of Winner Street, Paignton. The distant corner site of Osborne's store is now occupied by the Co-operative Society. In the foreground on the left, the Rocklight paraffin wagon is delivering to what was then Dellers stores.* Opposite page middle: *This picture of the Grand Hotel, Torquay sea front, was taken in 1880 not long after the building was completed.* Opposite page bottom: *Fleet Street, Torquay in 1890, looking towards the Strand. There were no trams in those days to interfere with horse-drawn transport.* Above: *The Grand Hotel, Torquay Sea Front about 1916. The overhead power for trams had replaced the Doulter system of power pick-up studs between the track. An early car can be seen in the forefront of the picture. Among the many distinguished visitors to the Grand was the famous novelist Agatha Christie.*

status of the English Riviera; the grandeur of Monte Carlo without the expense and bother of those early days of Continental travel.

Although some came by long-distance coach, the majority travelled by rail, the trains arriving frequently at Torquay and Paignton stations where they disgorged thousands of passengers, all ready to enjoy their annual one- or two-week holiday. During busy August Bank Holiday periods, hotels and guest houses were invariably fully booked. Families who simply took a chance of finding accommodation, discovered to their dismay there was nowhere to sleep. On those occasions it was not unusual to see many tired, exhausted and frustrated groups camping out on Torre Abbey and Paignton sands at night. As an example of the impact on the resort during the Bank Holiday period, Paignton's population would increase by as much as 25 000, creating a severe strain on water supplies and other services.

The increasing popularity of Torbay saw another important factor emerge. A growing number of regular visitors decided to sell their homes and to move to the westcountry to settle in one or the other of the three towns. The rise in the resident population was reflected in the comparative figures for the whole of Torbay from the census records of 1891 and 1969. In 1891 the total population was 49 000, but by 1969 had risen to 123 400.

Though many of the ancient buildings of Torbay disappeared as a result of the gentrification brought about by Victorian and Edwardian developers, many older parts of the town remained. The Old Manor Inn, Old Torquay Road, Paignton (top), was one of the oldest inns in the South West, dating back to the sixteenth century. The ladies cricket match (above) took place at Paignton in 1900. It was suggested for decency's sake that the batsmen should wear a longer skirt - her ankles were showing!

One of Torquay's finest nineteenth century buildings; the original Torbay Hospital in Higher Union Street, the foundation stone of which was laid in 1850 by His Imperial Highness Prince Peter of Oldenburg who was visiting the town at the time. This building, now Castle Chambers, served until the hospital near Lawes Bridge was opened in 1928. The board outside the hospital in this early 1900 photograph reads 'Supported by Voluntary Contributions'.

With the turn of the century, there came the miracle of wireless when, in 1901, Marconi transmitted a signal across the Atlantic. In the next ten years, with the improved efficiency and quality of motor cars, horse-drawn carriages were gradually replaced and, by 1908, the famous Wright brothers in America launched the conquest of the skies. Only a year later, in 1909, Louis Bleriot made the first cross-Channel flight to win the £1000 offered by the *Daily Mail*.

The dawn of the twentieth century prised open the lid of a whole repository of exciting new ideas and discoveries but while the world's great cities employed and exploited the new concepts, rural areas and seaside resorts adopted a more cautious approach.

Over the years, while many changes took place in the social life and development of the towns in Torbay, regrettably, not all were for the better. By wise and sometimes unwise decisions of alternating Town Councils, many former structures, highways and byways, dwellings and familiar landmarks have been demolished to give way to modernistic, remunerative ideas and architecture. The photographs shown here remind us of those 'yesterdays' when life was less frenetic, more meaningful and less covetous than today.

The following photograph (page 39) depicts the easy, relaxed, out-of-season atmosphere of Paignton shopping centre in 1905, when the resident population numbered only 7000. It shows the scene in Victoria Street, with the horse-cabs outside the premises of Waycotts Estate Agents (established in 1878). The al fresco butcher's display on the left is now occupied by the Abbey National Building Society.

The three boys shown on the left of the picture enjoyed the favourite pastime of bowling hoops. Some hoops were made of wood but the de luxe models were of iron. In the 1920s, a few shops

The centre of Paignton's shopping district in 1905.

In 1906, there were only five shops on the North side of Torbay Road from the junction of Garfield Road to the sea. They were Andrews' Stores, J. Sutton (printers), Coster's Photo Studio, the Misses Nichols and two half-shops Mme Florence (milliner) and Mr Trewin (hairdresser). Gradually more houses were converted into shops but there was none on the South side. By 1911 there were nine. Today Torbay Road is a busy place, with shops and arcades on both sides of the road.

along from the butchers, stood 'Valley's' famous sweet shop. It was not only a quality shop but an Alladin's cave of goodies where children gazed longingly at high shelves bearing gleaming glass jars filled with boiled sweets of every colour and shape; humbugs, gob stoppers, broken toffee bits and delicious sherbet.

Traffic was so scarce in those days that the two men in the forefront of the photograph with the barrow were able to settle down for a nice quiet chat. Today, their chances of survival would be slim indeed.

The styles originating in London swept the country and soon reached western resorts like Torquay. To gain the fullest advantage of the new vogue, the woman's body had to be streamlined into what was known as the hour-glass figure, where the bust and bottom were accentuated and the waist agonisingly compressed to a mere seventeen inches with the aid of tortuous corsetry.

Throughout the early 1900s many of these fashionably dressed ladies could be seen parading along the sea-front with their attendant male companions.

9 – By the Seaside

A major part of the attraction of Torbay to the early holidaymakers was the beach. Although at the turn of the century swimming had yet to become the popular pastime it is today, ladies and gentlemen would immerse themselves in the sea-water, emerging from bathing machines that lined the beach. These were often drawn down to the water's edge by horses.

Boating and bathing gave employment to many local people otherwise engaged in the, now declining, fishing industry. But specialist seaside entertainments also grew in popularity. Funfares with steam-driven merry-go-rounds, sand-sculptors, Punch & Judy shows, and donkey rides became regular attractions throughout Torbay's summer holiday period.

Top left: 'Sand artist', Daniel Anning, was well known for his wet sand sculptures at Torquay. His most famous figure was a Bengal tiger, but here is shown his sculpture of North Pole explorer, Doctor Cook. Top right: Grandmother and child at Torre Abbey sands, 1908. Above: Torquay Co-operative Society members on their annual children's outing on Torquay sands 28 August 1907.

THE BOOK OF TORBAY

Bathing machines line the shore at Corbyn's Head in the early 1900s. The huts were still operating on some of Torbay's beaches as late as the 1920s.

Children enjoying the simple pleasures of the seaside at Torre Abbey sands in the 1900s, sometime before the Collonade shelter was built.

Another view of the beach at Corbyn's Head. Boats for hire gave visitors the chance to row around the safe waters of the bay.

10 – Transport of Delight

Victoria Street, Paignton, 1909, viewed from Station Square with The Gerston Hotel on extreme right. The two ladies with their narrow-waisted long dresses reflect the fashion of the day, while the horse and carriage is in complete contrast to the new-fangled contraption of the GWR motor transport.

From 1904 onwards, the Ford Company of America produced thousands of their Model 'C' car, later to be nicknamed the 'Tin Lizzie', which was soon chugging its way along the roads of Torquay, Paignton and Brixham, much to the annoyance of 'cabbies' and die-hard Victorians who hurled a stream of abuse at these alien intruders of the new era. The friendly clip-clop of horse's hooves was usurped by the hostile roar and clatter of engines and the blare of motor-horns. Bristling retired colonels vehemently expressed their opinions in terms of 'the country is going to the dogs, sir'. But they were firmly convinced that this newfangled business would 'all come to nothing'.

The 'Tin Lizzie' and all other motor cars were painted black, falling in with the dictum of Henry Ford whose favourite maxim was 'you can have any colour you like as long as its black'. The Model 'T' car arrived in 1914 with the advantage of a retractable canvas hood, large headlamps, a glass windscreen and a bulb-press hooter.

In 1932, Ford produced the Model 'A' saloon with its steel bumpers and raucous klaxon horn. Although running boards were still a familiar feature, this model at the time was considered the cutting edge of technology.

As more cars arrived on the streets, more horse-drawn vehicles disappeared, and soon the pungent smell of horse-manure was replaced by the

Model 'C' Ford, the 'Tin Lizzie'.

The famous Model 'T' Ford.

poisonous reek of exhaust fumes. As competition in car manufacturing increased, so did the quantity and quality of production. Among the earlier appearances were the Morris Cowley, Morris Oxford, Austin Seven, and the Wolseley with its distinctive thermometer-topped bonnet.

The 1932 luxury Ford 'A' saloon.

Above: *Laying the tram lines near the hospital, 1907.*

Below: *An early excursion by tram in 1907. Note the curtained windows.*

Later, came the basic Trojan with its solid tyres. Unfortunately, the width of its axle happened to be the same as that of the trams which appeared in the streets of Torquay in 1907. Jokingly it was said of the Trojan that if its wheels caught in the tramlines the car would go straight to the depot.

The advent of the tram that year took Torquay by storm and the disruption created by the laying of the track brought normal trade almost to a standstill in some parts. The photo shown here gives some idea of the scale of the work that had to be carried out to establish a passenger service.

Laying tram lines near the old Town Hall where Fleet Street joins Union Street. Trams were in service from 1907 until 1934 when they were replaced by Devon General buses. During that period over 10 million passengers were carried.

The first trams were operated by a system of electric pads laid between the rails. Later, in 1911, the power was converted to a live overhead cable with contact through the tram's trolley arm. At each terminus, the conductor would use a rope to pull the arm around in the reverse direction. Such was the popularity of the tram that from 1907 to 1911, nearly one million passengers per year used the service.

The introduction of the charabanc which could take parties of around twenty to destinations further afield, brought an additional chance for the ordinary family to take day trips. It was certainly not a luxury ride for the vehicle was often open topped and therefore subject to all sorts of weather conditions, compelling passengers to protect themselves with mackintoshes, sou'westers and thick rugs. But there were few complaints and, if it rained, people put up with it and perhaps sang some of the songs then popular in the music-hall to keep up their spirits.

Among the popular tunes of the day were 'The Sheik of Araby.' 'If You Were the Only Girl in the World,' and 'Let the Great Big World Keep Turning' and 'Look for a Silver Lining.' Although it must be said, the unsmiling charabanc trippers in the photograph don't appear to have found that 'Silver Lining'.

The 'Scarlet Pimpernel' charabanc in the late 1920s. These trips would go as far afield as Dartmoor.

Paignton's Church Street charabanc awaits the last passenger, 1921.

THE BOOK OF TORBAY

TRANSPORT OF DELIGHT

The scenes in the following photographs recall the days before the motor car took over the streets of Torbay. The scenes, empty of cars, of wide avenues and tree-lined streets remind us of the elegance of the resort before the Great War.

Top: *Torquay seafront around 1908, showing the absence of traffic. The picture shows the Gardener's Cottage overlooked by what became Rock Walk. Although the trams had arrived, as shown by the lines, the cabbies still maintained a presence.*
Bottom: *The Strand showing the clock tower and Vane Hill.*

THE BOOK OF TORBAY

TRANSPORT OF DELIGHT

Top: *This turn of the century photograph of Torwood street shows horse-drawn vehicles much in evidence, the exception being the bicycle. The trees have long since gone. The photographer would have been standing close to where the Strand clock tower now is.*

Right: *Torquay Strand prior to 1902 and before the Strand clock tower was built. The building on the left shows part of Williams & Cox, furnishers and undertakers. The store was burned down in 1939 and rebuilt and taken over by Hoopers.*

Below: *Paignton's Palace Avenue in 1908. In those days there was little need for the traffic lights which now operate at the distant junction of Victoria Street and Totnes Road.*

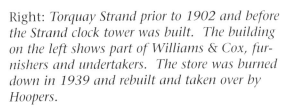

45

TRANSPORT OF DELIGHT

Old Mill Road, Chelston, as it was in the 1900s.

The cab-stand at Wellswood in 1905. This was an elegant residential area even at the turn of the century.

TRANSPORT OF DELIGHT

Lower Union Street, Torquay c. 1910. Abbey Roads branches away (unseen) to the left.

Union Street, Torquay, in 1903, looking towards Higher Union Street. On the right is the porticoed entrance of the Union Hotel, built in 1831.

TRANSPORT OF DELIGHT

One of Cawdle's coaching excursions setting off from Torquay in 1906. There are no fewer than eighteen people aboard which meant that the horses had to haul over a ton of human cargo up over the steep Devon hills.

These four ladies are admiring the unrestricted views from Marine Drive, as it was in 1912.

11 – High Days and Holidays

The long reign of Queen Victoria gave her subjects plenty of opportunity to celebrate various jubilees. Indeed the Victorians might be said to have made nationwide celebrations a national pastime. Not a war ended, nor a royal event passed, without the people coming out on the streets in wild revelry. Church bells were rung, beacons lit, and bonfires built to light up the evening skies.

In Torbay these national events were supplemented by local celebrations such as the regattas, carnivals and annual fairs, and where these took place in the holiday season holidaymakers swelled the jubilant crowds, and local tradesmen made hay while the sun shone. All this added to the attraction of Torbay as a resort and, though more genteel in past times, many of these events have continued to the present day.

Top: *An elegant float entry in one of Torquay's Carnivals in the early 1900s. In the background are shops of the period at the harbourside along Victoria Parade. Their names will no doubt be familiar to many Torquinians: Repik the furriers, Douglas's Restaurant, Burridge's florist, and Sermons watches & jewellery.*
Bottom: *King's Drive Gardens near Torquay seafront on opening day in April 1905.*

THE BOOK OF TORBAY

HIGH DAYS AND HOLIDAYS

Torre Abbey grounds, Empire Day, 24 May 1905. This children's festival marked the occasion of Queen Victoria's birthday and the achievements of the British Empire during her long reign. Note the black choir at the centre of the picture.

Empire Day, and the children sing grace before high tea begins.

THE BOOK OF TORBAY

HIGH DAYS AND HOLIDAYS

Torquay Regatta fairground on a misty day in 1906. The archway carries an advert for 'Hancock's Living Pictures', possibly a magic lantern show.

Crowds gather at Queen's Park, Paignton, on 28 February 1907. The event appears to be some sort of military tattoo. Queen's Park was well known for its cricket matches, archery contests and athletic events.

THE BOOK OF TORBAY

HIGH DAYS AND HOLIDAYS

Paignton Sands in 1913. Deck chairs, ice creams and donkey rides – what more could one want?

An unusual picture of Goodrington Sands about 1912. For those who could afford it, a launch service ran from Paignton beach to Goodrington Sands, then known as a select retreat. The triangular Langford's tents were quite a novel feature and did service as beach huts.

THE BOOK OF TORBAY

HIGH DAYS AND HOLIDAYS

A family and the dog gather for tea on Paignton Sands in the summer of 1910. The shore end of the pier is just visible in the background.

Well Street, Paignton, in 1909, appears quiet and uneventful, but the flag in the window on the left and the gathering of the children suggests another celebration is underway. Today, a constant stream of traffic flows through this little street. As its name suggests, the street had a communal well serving the local community. It is believed to have served as the only water supply as late as 1863.

THE BOOK OF TORBAY

HIGH DAYS AND HOLIDAYS

This picture of Oddicombe Beach in 1904 shows several bathing machines but few bathers. The rough seas suggest it was a windy and rather uncomfortable day for swimming.

In contrast to the picture above, this photo shows a placid, comfortable sea for swimming at Oddicombe Beach in 1903. Note the voluminous costumes the ladies are wearing, one with a sailor's collar.

THE BOOK OF TORBAY

HIGH DAYS AND HOLIDAYS

Regatta Day swimming and diving events at Torquay Pier, 1904. A large crowd have turned up to watch the programme which was always promoted by the Torquay Leander Swimming and Life Saving Society. The temporary diving stage is shown at the left of the picture. An interesting variety of transport waits for customers.

A 1908 view of the sea road at Meadfoot before it was developed into its present appearance.

A fine two-masted schooner lies secure at the habour wall, Victoria Parade about the year 1906.

Torquay Regatta 1908 showing the harbourside fairground on Victoria Parade. The slatted wooden trays (far left) indicate a coconut shie stall.

12 – The Home Fleet in Torbay

The arrival of the Home Fleet in Torbay in 1910 was brought about more by freak weather conditions than any other reason. On Saturday 23 July of that year the combined Atlantic, Mediterranean and Home Fleets, under the command of Admiral Sir William May GCVO KCB, in the battleship HMS *Dreadnought,* were ordered to assemble at Mount's Bay, Penzance. A large bay indeed, but wide open to extreme weather conditions. There they waited pending the arrival of His Majesty King George V, to review the fleet.

Beautiful weather prevailed as the 230 ships of all types (including 37 large battleships) assembled in the English channel and sailed into Mount's Bay where they dropped anchor in their usual precise fashion. Unfortunately, that night there arose a gale the like of which had not been experienced for years.

At the first signs of the storm the smaller craft of the fleet got under way and scurried to the haven of Penzance Dock, but as the afternoon wore on the tempest increased in ferocity, posing a serious question for Admiral May. Finally he made his decision and gave the order for the fleets to weigh anchor and steam for the shelter of Torbay.

Cornwall's loss was Devon's gain for on the Monday morning the people of Torbay awoke to find that the usual blue waters of the bay had turned dark grey with a concentration of warships lying at anchor. News of the revised venue for the Royal Review spread throughout Torbay and the country around and hurried arrangements were made in hopeful anticipation of the visit of the Royal family.

His Majesty King George V had ascended the throne following the death of his father, King Edward VII, just two months earlier. Known as the 'Sailor King' because of his previous service in the Royal Navy and his love for the sea and ships, George V became Admiral of the greatest and most powerful fleet that ever sailed.

It was originally planned that the sovereign should board the royal yacht *Victoria and Albert* at Spithead, then sail to Mount's Bay to review the fleet on the Monday, but Queen Mary was known to be a poor sailor and it was therefore decided to delay the journey until the storm had abated.

His Majesty King George V.

The royal yacht, escorted by cruisers, finally left the Solent on Tuesday 26 July, and sailed for Torbay. The yacht, with her escort in line astern, arrived at 4pm and, as they reached the outer limits of the bay, people lining cliff-top vantage points could see the King, in his uniform as Admiral of the Fleet, standing to attention on the bridge. Behind him stood Queen Mary and their two young children, Prince George and Princess Mary. The Union flag flew at the mizzen mast, the King's Admiral's flag at the foremast and the Royal Standard the mainmast. Royal Marines lining the decks of the ships presented arms while ensigns were dipped in salute as the bands played the National Anthem.

The yacht passed through the lines of warships and anchored just off Torquay in full view of the many sightseers. Their Majesties were shortly joined by their eldest son ,His Royal Highness The Prince of Wales who, at the time, was serving in the Royal Navy at Dartmouth Training College. The King's uncle, The Duke of Connaught, also joined the royal party having travelled by train from London.

THE BOOK OF TORBAY

Top and bottom: *View of the combined fleet at anchor in Torbay, July 1910.* Centre: *The royal yacht* Victoria and Albert *on which the royal party sailed into the bay in order to inspect the fleet at anchor.*

THE BOOK OF TORBAY

During the 1914-18 war famous newspaper artists sometimes contributed their drawings and sketches to naval and army men who were in the forefront of the fighting. Those shown here, and in the section on the Great War, are copies in miniature of the originals which were presented to the author's father in 1915/16. Those shown, clockwise from top left, are by Starwood, Leo Cheney, Bert Monkro and Alfred Leeze.

On the Wednesday morning the King and the Prince of Wales joined Admiral May aboard HMS *Dreadnought* and it was intended the fleet would put to sea for gunnery practice and manoeuvres. Once again the weather took a hand, when a thick haze over the sea, which shortly turned to rain, prevented the ships from sailing.

To pass the time, the King and his son took the opportunity of exploring the modern, most powerful and revolutionary battleship ever built by any navy. Later in the day visibility improved sufficiently for the ships to practice their gunnery further out in the English Channel. *Dreadnought* fired a number of salvoes at a target towed by HMS *Isis* five miles away and the King congratulated the gunners on their shooting. Then, much to the consternation of senior officers he expressed a wish to fire the guns himself. Every possible check was made to ensure his safety before he was permitted to enter the gun turret where he successfully fired five rounds at the target.

The spectacle of the fleet's return, as witnessed from the high land was very imposing. When the mass of ships were sighted they were smothered in smoke. As it cleared it was seen that there were eight columns of ships with eight in each column, sixty four in all, arranged in lines as they had been disposed throughout the week in Torbay, each led by its flagship.

The ships kept station with admirable precision. The majestic spectacle of between four and five square miles of battleships and big cruisers, proceeding at about 14 knots in perfect formation, amply rewarded those who had journeyed to watch from the shore. At exactly 2.30pm, the signal was made from *Dreadnought* to anchor and for toher ships to moor in their order. On the signal being hauled down, sixty-four anchors dropped as one, with the second anchors being let go similarly by signal.

Of special interest to the King during those moments of signalling activity were the orders given by the Flag Officer standing at his side on the bridge announcing the signal orders to be relayed to the rest of the fleet. As the armada approached its respective anchorages, speed had to be reduced to a mere 5 knots. The signal for 'speed' in those days was the pennant 'G' for George. As the officer announced 'George 5 Hoist' and moments later 'George 5 Execute', His Majesty is said to have visibly winced but made no comment.

Meanwhile, that intrepid aviator Mr Grahame-White, undeterred by the unstable weather conditions, took off from Torre Abbey in his bi-plane and flew over the fleet, diving and weaving to demonstrate the manoeuverability of his aircraft, paying special attention to HMS *Dreadnought*, circling the mighty warship several times before flying further out in the bay across many of the other warships.

His flight lasted more than twelve minutes and, to the cheers of the spectators, he made a perfect landing back at Torre Abbey meadows. Grahame-White repeated his act that evening when the ships returned to the bay from their manoeuvres and it was estimated that a crowd of over 20 000 watched this second exhibition of flying. The King was reported to have been greatly impressed by the skill of the aviator.

A number of far-sighted spectators of the flights noted that £100 million worth of warships, no less than sixteen admirals, including the Commander-in-Chief and Vice Admiral Prince Louis of Battenburg in the battleship HMS *Exmouth,* and 50 000 officers and men, had all been at the mercy of one man in an aeroplane as the fleet lay powerless beneath him. Although it would appear that the fleet's gunners, purely as an exercise, tried to train their guns on the plane, it was found that the guns could not be elevated sufficiently to target it. The significance of this came as a shock to the Admiralty for it revealed all too clearly the vulnerability of warships in any future war to this new threat from the air.

It would have been an embarrassing moment for the First Lord of the Admiralty, Lord Fisher, if he had been present, for it was he who was responsible for the defence capability of the British Fleet.

Thirty-one years later, the truth of this was tragically demonstrated when, on 8 December 1941, Japanese bombers swept down on the United States naval base at Pearl Harbor and sank the entire anchored American fleet including eight battleships in less than ninety minutes.

Friday was the day the people of Devon, and Torbay in particular, had been waiting for. It had

Aviator Graham-White preparing to take off from Torre Abbey meadows in his biplane in July 1910. He was later to fly over the assembled Atlantic, Home and Mediterranean Fleets in Torbay.

been made known during the week that His Majesty the King would come ashore to return to London by train. Long before the royal party stepped on to the aptly named Princess Pier, crowds had gathered along the route to Torquay station. The King was met by the Mayor and other dignitaries of the Borough Council and, after a short address in which he stated his regret at being unable to spend longer in the beautiful resort, the King and his family were driven to the station to the cheers of the flag-waving crowds.

After the royal train had left on its journey to London the crowds returned their attention to the warships which were now preparing to sail. Soon the summer sky became blackened by smoke from the funnels of the coal-burning ships. One by one they lifted their moorings and moved silently out of the bay.

So the momentous events of the week came to a close and, for a while, the crowds wandered around aimlessly; the King had gone, the gallant aviator had gone and now the last warship had slipped over the horizon. All that remained were the memories of those who were privileged to have witnessed the 'Greatest Show on Earth', knowing that Britannia ruled the waves.

A postcard celebrating the Royal Review at Torbay by King George V in September 1910.

The Daily Mail *Avro flies over the Hotel Redcliffe.*

The Daily Mail *pilot Raynham in his floatplane, takes off from Preston Sands in 1914.*

13 – Flights of Fancy

The flight over the combined fleet was one in a series of early flying exploits that took place in Torbay. In the spring of 1914, the *Daily Mail* airmen Salmet and Raynham gave exhibition flights round the bay in their Avro machine. This had no retractable undercarriage and, as they were coming in to land, onlookers recalled that the wheels sometimes scraped the tops of bushes where the Festival Hall now stands. As a consequence, spectators on the green had to run for their lives. The small boy on the left of the aircraft (circled) is Frank Baker standing behind his father Percy Baker, well known to old Paigntonians. Frank's elder brother Jack, became the town's impressario, starting with marionettes and progressing to pantomime productions.

Frank Baker, while a small boy in Torquay, stands next to the Daily Mail *aircraft that gave exhibition flights over Torbay during the early months of 1914.*

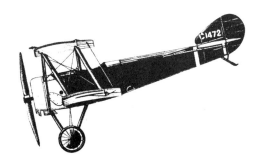

The makeshift wooden theatre stage erected on the Green where now houses stand in Berry Square.

Paignton Dramatic Society and the cast from 'The Rising Generation' produced at Christmas 1926. Left-right: John Sutton of Suttons Printers, Greta Huggins, Rex Axworthy of Axworthy Stationers, Maidee Stevens, Leo Foale, Fred Smart, Marion Smart, and Mrs Loring.

Below: *The cast of Charles Heslop's 'The Brownies' at the Paignton Adelphi, 1919.*

14 – Paignton: In on the Act

Some Paigntonians will remember Fred Spencer's popular al fresco concert party by the Pier. Compared with modern entertainment facilities the going was certainly tough, as the artistes had to sing and perform in the open air, without microphones while competing for attention against all the background noises of the seafront. The only means of revenue were the coppers charged for sitting in a deck chair, but when it rained the audience ran for shelter and the crowd usually started to melt away as soon as one of the party came around with a collection box.

Just before the Great war, Fred Spencer was unable to obtain his usual stand on the Green and transferred to a piece of waste land behind Torbay Road. The wooden stage shown in the photograph (opposite top) was sited where the six houses in Berry Square now stand. Marcus Bridgman built twelve houses opposite and called them Kernou Road.

The next step in Paignton's pre-1914 summer entertainment was the opening of the Adelphi Gardens situated in the road of that name, the enclosed wooden and canvas pavilion being sited where a block of flats now stand. This of course was an innovation as entrance was by ticket only (canvas chairs one-shilling-and-sixpence and one shilling; slatted seats at the rear sixpence). Almost overnight, Max Cardiff and his 'Glad Idlers' soared to local fame, drawing packed houses during the season, with the audience invariably greeting the rising of the curtain with a burst of applause. There were of course no microphones or amplifiers in those days.

AMATEUR THEATRICALS

Early in the war, musician Hubert Kiver joined the East Surrey Regiment went to France and was promptly killed. Elsie April, a brilliant pianist, subsequently became the famous C.B. Cochran's musician-in-chief. After the war the Adelphi Gardens were leased to Charles Heslop who, in 1919, opened his show 'The Brownies' which included his wife Maidee Field. This very popular entertainment returned for several seasons.

Charles Heslop continued a successful career appearing in many London shows including

The 'Glad Idlers' concert party. Left-right back: *C. Andrews; Phyllis Beden; Hubert Kiver.* Front: *Miss Ord; Max Cardiff; Elsie April.*

'Paganini' with Richard Tauber and Evelyn Laye. He also played with Wilfred Hyde-White, Margaret Leighton and, in 1966, at the age of 81, he appeared in his last stage show 'The Diplomatic Baggage' at the Wyndhams.

During the 1920s and early 30s, the Paignton Dramatic Society regularly produced stage plays at Christmas and Easter. These included 'Tilly of Bloomsbury', 'The Man who Stayed at Home', Hawleys of the High Street', 'The Young Person in Pink', 'The Crime at Blossoms', 'The Ghost Train', 'A Pair of Silk Stockings' and 'Outward Bound'.

Paignton Pantomime Productions, still successfully running in 1977, arose from the ashes of the 'Paignton Pudding' which Jack Baker produced for the Coronation in 1935, packing the Public Hall for a fortnight.

Torquay's Royal Theatre, traditional home of Pantomimes had just been sold for cinema conversion and made Torquay's theatrical prospect for Christmas 1935 bleak indeed. But Jack Baker again rallied the 'Pudding' team, secured guarantees from local businessmen and, encouraged by the Council's legacy of 'Pudding' scenery, made the big decision to stage the show. In their 25 years of productions the Society donated many thousands of pounds to charities.

The Jubilee Arch at the end of Torbay Road, Paignton.

THE PAIGNTON JUBILEE ARCH. 1935.

This wooden latticed arch was constructed at the seaward end of Torbay Road to mark the occasion of the Silver Jubilee of King George V and Queen Mary in 1935. It was illuminated by hundreds of electric light bulbs installed by the Paignton Electric Company. It remained as a tourist attraction until 1936 when the King died, following a twenty-five year reign, from 1910 to 1936.

PAIGNTON COLLEGE

In the years before the Great War, Hyde Road was entirely residential and all the houses sedate private residences with one exception. Midway along this quiet road stood Paignton College, Edwardian in style but designed and built as a school with a fine well-kept lawn running from the entrance gate to the headmaster's residence. There was a traditional belfry and a spacious area at the rear. This private school was run on grammar school lines by Brantford Hartland.

Only those who lived in pre-war 1914 Paignton will be able to recall the building in its original form as the site is now occupied by the Crossways Shopping Centre. The property adjoining the school was Newstead House, occupied by Dr Newman Collier, and now part of the Post Office complex.

15 – Dellers Café

Old Paigntonians will remember Dellers Café of Torbay Road, Paignton, with affection, and the outstanding contribution it made to the social life of the town. In 1910 a Plymouth builder imported the distinctive bricks from Holland and Sweden but the actual building took a considerable time due to early difficulties with the foundations.

The night before the café was opened to the public in 1911 the owner, Mr W. Lambshead, invited many Paigntonians to a reception. It must be remembered that in those days the town was compact and small with a population around 9000, so that the addition of so grand and imposing a building was hailed as a great innovation.

The café soon became a social centre, not only for residents, but for those living in nearby towns who were attracted by the congenial surroundings and the novelty of music provided by a trio. The summer months saw holidaymakers queuing to get tables, and tea-time on Saturday afternoons was particularly popular with out-of-town shoppers who, along with cadets from Britannia Royal Naval College at Dartmouth, came to be seen at one of the region's most fashionable venues. During the winter there was a succession of whist drives, dinners and dances, arranged by club secretaries and many local orgnisations. The outstanding event was the New Year's Eve party, tickets for which had to be bought many weeks in advance. The Rotary Club of Paignton met well over 2000 times up to its last weekly lunch on 30 September 1965, when President Leslie Rossiter and its members said goodbye to Dellers.

The elegance of Dellers Café is seen in this photograph taken from Torbay Road, Paignton.

The grand entrance to Dellers Café, 1930.

Torbay Road with Dellers Café just visible at the foot of the road on the right.

In 1941 a special party attended by over a thousand people, and organised by the Paignton Parish Church, was held at Dellers Café. The photograph shows a small section of those who attended. It includes: Rev B. Montague Dale, Vicar of Paignton Parish Church; Rev. Ryder Jones, Curate of Paignton Parish Church and Mrs Jones; Mr E.S. Riley, vicar's warden and Mrs Riley; Mr and Mrs W. Coysh, owners of the Church St and Hyde Road Post Offices and the Toy Shop in Victoria St; Mrs Pugh, owner of the pram shop opposite Victoria Park; Mrs Martin, owner of the outfitters shop in Church Street; Mrs and Miss Mathews, owners of the butcher's shop in Winner Street; Mrs Maunder, owner of the general grocers, Southfield Road; Miss Peggy Thorne, Senior Librarian, Paignton Library; Miss J. Western, bakers & confectioners in Church Street.

16 – Cinema Entertainment in Torbay

The first cinema opened in 1909 as a part of the market and was given the name of 'Picturedrome'. Two years later in 1911, a second cinema appeared called the 'Electric', but renamed the 'Colony' in 1962. The 'Empire' opened its doors in 1912 and the 'Tudor,' in St Marychurch, in 1929. Another cinema the 'Burlington' had its premiere in 1920.

Torquay's most modern cinema, the 'Regal' at Castle Circus made its debut in 1933. The Odeon cinema in Abbey Road, which also opened in 1933, is still in business and has an historic and long tradition. It was originally opened on 10 April 1880 as the Royal Theatre and Opera House.

The first Chairman of the new theatre was Mr W. F. Splatt JP, and the opening performance that night was 'Who's your friend.' In 1930, the celebrated playwright and author, John Galsworthy, was asked to write a Foreword to the theatre's Jubilee programme, a copy of which is produced overleaf.

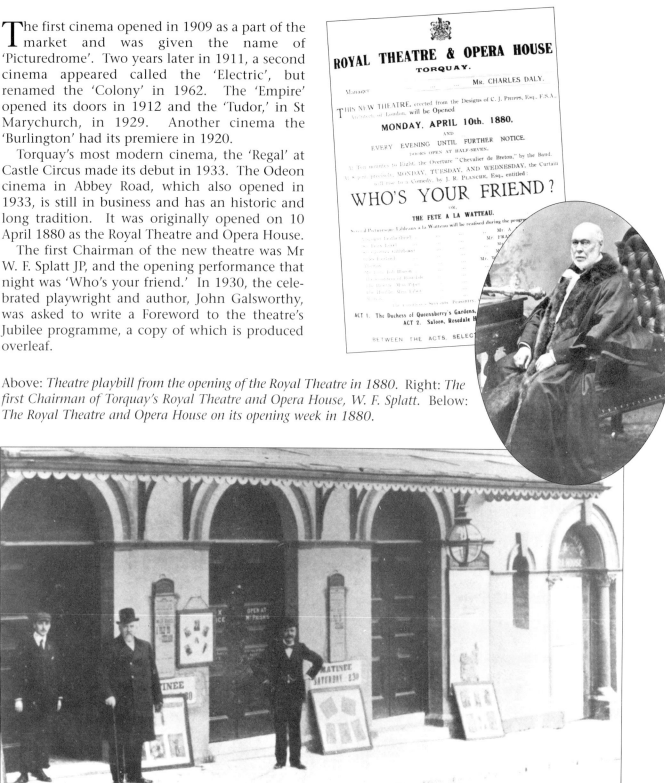

Above: *Theatre playbill from the opening of the Royal Theatre in 1880.* Right: *The first Chairman of Torquay's Royal Theatre and Opera House, W. F. Splatt.* Below: *The Royal Theatre and Opera House on its opening week in 1880.*

> PRESUMABLY, I am asked to write this foreword to the Jubilee Programme, because this Torquay Theatre is the only one I have disgraced by a personal performance. In the early nineties some hardy amateurs here played Gilbert's "Engaged," and to me fell the part of "Symperson." So far as I recollect, I had side-whiskers, light trousers, a daughter and stage fright.
>
> Those were simple and palmy days for the professional stage. No films no revues, ballets, or radio; save the music hall, not a rival in the field. And take them all round, weren't the plays of that period bad! And yet, I expect, they were much better than in the days of my father's youth in Plymouth. Galleryites at that time were very plain-spoken. I remember him telling me of a night when some one in the Gallery there had made himself so unpleasant that there were shouts of "throw him over, throw him over!" till an Irish voice was heard above the din "Aisy there! don't waste um, kill a fiddler wid um!"
>
> To-day we are all so well-behaved that even authors are safe — more or less.
>
> I know I express the feelings of Torquay when I hail these immemorial boards on this their Jubilee, and wish them many a stout performance yet.
>
> JOHN GALSWORTHY.
>
> Bury House,
> Bury, nr. Pulborough,
> Sussex.
> April 5th, 1930.

Above left: *Galsworthy's foreword to the Jubilee theatre programme.*

Above Right: *Patrons arriving at the Theatre in the 1920s.*

Left: *A queue forms in front of the Electric Cinema in Union Lane, Torquay where one of the most popular films of 1941 'How Green Was My Valley', was showing.*

Below: *The Odeon Cinema in Torquay at its opening in 1933.*

17 – Torquay's Famous Pavilion

Torquay Pavilion c. 1912. The posters advertise symphony concerts and a lecture by the celebrated Norwegian artctic explorer Roald Amundsen who had, in 1911, successfully raced Scott to the South Pole.

Along with the Marine Spa ballroom, Torquay's other citadel of entertainment was the splendid Torquay Pavilion. Built in the style of George IV, it was opened on 10 August 1912, some twenty years after the idea of a Pavilion was first discussed by the local authority. It was built on land partly reclaimed from the sea and constructed on a concrete raft on which a framework of steel stanchions and girders was erected. The impressive central copper-covered dome is topped with a full-sized figure of Britannia with two smaller domes at each side of the entrance surmounted by copper figures of Mercury, the messenger and god of eloquence.

Its formal opening was acclaimed in the national press as 'Torquay's Palace of Pleasure'. Inside - was a foyer and an auditorium with lounges, along with a splendid café. Its interior exuded an atmosphere of elegance with its oak panelling, moulded plasterwork, carved balcony, stained glass, and potted palms. Outside was an open air promenade and tea garden.

The town then took the important step of founding a municipal orchestra of 25 players under the musical direction of Basil Hindenberg (later to be known as Basil Cameron) who, for an annual salary of £500, was expected to produce 500 symphony concerts every twelve months. He conducted the Torquay Municipal Orchestra at the opening ceremony.

Right from the start there was a problem. The Pavilion café, where waitresses in cinnamon-brown frocks and frilly caps served hot lunches at one shilling and sixpence, and dinner at two shillings and sixpence, was a busy place. It also adjoined the auditorium and, to the annoyance of concert-goers, the musicians were accompanied by the banging of cups and saucers and the jingle of teaspoons. Eventually a glass screen was installed at a cost of £650.

Over the years many famous performers appeared at the Pavilion, including Paul Robeson, Dame Nellie Melba, John McCormack, Sid James and Morecombe and Wise. On the negative side the Pavilion faced financial problems from time to time and there were occasions when the building lost money and was considered by some to be a 'white elephant.

Over the years, the entertainment changed from classical concerts to military bands, films, plays and concert parties. In 1930, a grand musical festival was held by Ernest Goss, conductor and musical director since 1920. Guest conductors were Sir Edward Elgar, Sir Landon Ronald, Sir Henry Wood, Sir Malcolm Sergeant, Sir Thomas Beecham, Sir Adrian Boult, Sir Hamilton Harty, Eric Coates and John Barbirolli.

Notable artists included Clifford Curzon, Schnabel, Leon Goussons, Mark Hamburg, Cyril Smith, Moiseiwitch, Isobel Baillie, Maura Lymphany, Radrich and Lander, Stamford Robinson, Dame Ethel Smythe, Fritz Kreisler and Richard Tauber.

The building's financial ups and downs continued throughout the Second World War and after. Attractions in the 1950s included the Fol de Rols,

Above: *Potted palms flank the Pavilion staircase in 1925, reflecting an atmosphere of opulence and elegance.*

Left: *One of the many Pavilion concerts held in the 1953-54 seasons. The singer is believed to be the well-known artiste Elizabeth James.*

Torquay Municipal Orchestra, 1930, with its conductor Ernest Goss.

Twinkle, and the Gang Show. In April 1953 the Municipal Orchestra gave its final concert.

In 1961 the Princess Theatre opened and less than a year later the council were considering the possibility of redeveloping the Pavilion site. The spectre of demolition loomed and, by the 1970s, was a strong probability. Only one year later the beloved Marine Spa was pulled down to make way for what some described as an 'architectural monstrosity' called Coral Island.

The loss of the Marine Spa caused considerable anger and indignation in the town, especially when at the same time money was pouring out on the development of the Beacon site. It looked as though the Pavilion would be the next to fall to the bulldozer but in the nick of time help arrived in the shape of a remarkable group called Friends of the Pavilion led by Mrs Sheila Hardaway.

They were determined to save what they called 'a place of many memories, a unique achievement and design, representing the heart of Torquay.' They found heartfelt support and today the Pavilion is a listed building, looking forward to another century of service to the town.

THE BOOK OF TORBAY

TRANQUIL RETREATS

A fine view of a tranquil Torquay seafront in 1909. The tram on the right had still not entirely taken over from horse-drawn traffic

A quiet day on Babbacombe Downs for this Edwardian gentleman, seated by the deserted bandstand.

18 – Torbay in the Great War

In July 1914, the tense European situation had reached a point when most people were convinced that war was imminent. Germany, under the leadership of Kaiser Wilhelm of Austria who wanted war and was determined to have it, marched into Belgium in a bid to subdue France, to whom Britain had pledged support. The first three days of August saw intense diplomatic activity, but late on the evening of 4 August, it was announced that Britain was at war.

A few units of the Home Fleet were in Torbay at the time and that night, sailors were hastily rounded up from the local pubs by naval patrol police and and ordered back to their ships. The announcement of war cast a gloom over the Torquay Regatta weekend. Inevitable conscription would mean husbands being parted from wives, fathers from children and many a promising career ruined. Those already on holiday, anxious to get home, found trains filled with regular and reserve soldiers and sailors speeding back to headquarters. There were of necessity many cancelled holidays which had a devastating effect on Torbay hoteliers. There was also a sudden absence of coastguards from harbours, men who were registered as Royal Fleet Reservists. Local Territorials. were also called to arms.

A wartime cartoon by Cravenham - a caricature of Kaiser Wilhelm II - the Hun as a wild boar.

In those early war years, as the magnitude of the battles on the fields of Flanders increased, and the slaughter of thousands of British soldiers continued, so was the impact felt in Torbay. With trainloads of wounded arriving, there was urgent need for hospital accommodation and, by the beneficence of the owner of Oldway Mansion,

Kaiser Wilhelm II

Field Marshal Sir Douglas Haig, Commander-in-Chief of the British forces.

Oldway, taken in 1914 during its use by the American Women's War Relief organisation as a military hospital.

Paris Singer, the magnificent building was placed at the disposal of the American Women's Organisation and equipped as a hospital containing over 200 beds.

This greatly supplemented the Town Hall's hospital accommodation of 50 beds while smaller, private hospitals were established at 'Rockwood', 'The Manor House', 'Stoodley Knowle' 'Lyncourt', 'Royden' and 'Fairfield'.

In the early months of the war national recruitment went on without the need for conscription. Thousands of young men joined up in a state of patriotic excitement, hell-bent on getting into the fight 'before it was all over by Christmas' as they first thought. They had no idea of the horror awaiting them in the trenches. Little did they know that it was to be four long years and four bloody Christmases before it would all be over.

At that time thousands of men were marching off to France singing the lines from the popular song:

'Goodbyee, goodbyee, lady dear wipe a tear from your eye—ee. Though its hard to part I know, I'll be tickled to death to go'.

Other popular marching songs at that time were 'Pack up your troubles in your old kit bag' and 'Its a long way to Tipperary.' In Music Halls the songs of Sir Harry Lauder caught the imagination of the public and were endlessly played on the new-fangled wind-up gramophones.

Torquay hospitality to thousands of wounded soldiers from the battlefields of France was made priority. A picture taken outside the Pavilion in 1915 shows convalescent soldiers about to enjoy an outing in open cars. Crowds have gathered to see them and the vehicles shown include cars, horse-drawn carriages, a tram, bicycles and a motorbike and sidecar. Several babies can be seen among the crowd and people are packed into one of the Pavilion bandstands for a better view.

At home the war was developing into a subtle campaign of Government propaganda. Factory workers were faced with large posters of General Kitchener pointing an accusatory finger with the

Harrison's cartoon parodying the call for scrap iron to aid the war effort.

THE BOOK OF TORBAY

The scene outside Torquay Pavilion in 1915. Convalescent soldiers are being taken on a tour of the town in open cars while citizens of the town line the streets to cheer them. Disillusioned by the jingoism and the ignorance of those at home to the realities of the horrors of the Western Front, many soldiers found these celebrations almost unbearable and longed to get back to the comradeship of their pals in the trenches.

words 'Your Country Needs You.' Girls ran along the streets pinning white feathers on those men not wearing uniforms, charging them with cowardice. One famous London playwright (a large fat man) was accosted by one of these girls: 'Why aren't you out at the front?' to which he replied, 'My dear young lady, if you'll kindly walk around to the side, you'll see I am!'

The bitter character of the war showed its ugly face from the end of 1914 when German cruisers sailed across the North Sea and shelled towns on the north-east coast. German Zeppelins attacked London and their army used mustard gas for the first time in France. Most shocking of all, and ultimately instrumental in bringing the USA into the war, a German submarine sank the neutral American liner *Lusitania*.

The notorious battle of the Somme opened on 1 July 1916 following a week-long artillery bombardment of German positions. IN one day the

Cartoons by 'Toy', Bruce Bairnsfather and Heath Robinson make fun of various naval situations of the Great War.

77

THE BOOK OF TORBAY

Men of the 2nd sub-Division Field Ambulance marching along Torbay Road, Paignton, in 1915.

Many South Devon men joined the Royal Marines who were a vital part of Britain's fighting force. Charles Crombie's cartoon wishes them good luck.

British suffered 57 400 casualties, of which 20 000 were killed.

The trench warfare in France developed into a four-year-long haemorrhage of the lifeblood of the nation. Flanders became killing fields of blood, mud, shellfire and lice. 'Going over the top' often meant almost certain death and thousands were mown down by murderous enemy gunfire in a matter of minutes; whole battalions were wiped out trying to win a few yards of ground.

Military historians claim there was little strategic warcraft or tactical skill applied by the Commander-in-Chief, Sir Douglas Haig, in the terrible battles of Ypres, the Marne and Passchendaele. Some assert that men were being shovelled into the cauldron of fire in the hope the enemy would run out of ammunition. The 1914-1918 war resulted in a world death toll of nearly 15 million.

In Torbay the appearance of so many young men had a marked effect on the social life and economy. Following their days of training and drilling at Ellacombe, and at Paignton Green, these recruits would invade the towns making a marked impression, financially and otherwise, on shopkeepers and publicans, especially those at the relatively isolated sea-end of Torbay Road.

Paignton rose to the occasion and looked after its military visitors with kindness and consideration, most being billeted in private houses. The YMCA and local churches also organised hospitality which was just the kind of help young men, recently enlisted and away from home, most needed.

Relatives of wounded soldiers recuperating at Oldway came to Paignton in large numbers by train, and this made the resort even better known

This photograph of a YMCA group was taken in the grounds of Dellers Café in 1916. Civilian members of the YMCA and lady helpers included: front row left to right: *Mr G. Bridgeman, Miss E. German, Mrs Bootyman, Mr F. Rockett, Miss L. Beare, Miss M.Sutton, Mr F. Collins.* Second row: *Mr A. E. Knight, Miss Lampton, J. Sutton, Mrs Crouch, Mrs Bridgeman, Miss Bootyman, Miss Harris and Mr A. J. Brabner.*

An old salt, from a wartime cartoon by Will Owen. In fact many fishermen served in the Merchant and Royal Navy, whilst a large number of trawlers were commandered to act as armed vessels on anti-submarine and minelaying work.

in the large cities of the Midlands and North of England.

Such was the carnage of the battlefront that, at home, there was an acute shortage of men to work in factories and on farms. Women were thus appealed to, to take on the positions traditionally occupied by men. This later was to have a profound effect on the place of women in the social order who proved themselves more than capable of taking the place of men in the workplace.

On 31 May 1916, the famous Battle of Jutland took place off the Denmark coast. It was one of the greatest sea battles in history when the giant battleships of the British Grand Fleet slogged it out with the German High Seas Fleet. Both suffered heavy losses in this indecisive engagement, but in the following months it was the Royal Navy's blockade that helped to bring Germany to the brink of starvation, her navy to mutiny and the war to an end.

On 11 November 1918, Germany's request for armistice was granted, but the allies required her to surrender her entire fleet. On 22 November the British Grand Fleet sailed for the last time, escorting the entire German fleet into Scapa Flow

THE BOOK OF TORBAY

Four of these Great War British 'Tommies' are wearing German military headgear, collected from dead or captured enemy soldiers.

The arrival of a thousand members of the Royal Army Medical Corps in 1915 had a startling effect on the local economy and on social life in the area, making up for a little of the revenue lost to the cancellation of holidays during the war. This scene is at Ellacombe Green.

THE BOOK OF TORBAY

Ceremonial entry into Mons, 1918, with units of the London Scottish and the London Rifle Brigade taking part. Included in the photograph is LRB member J. Sutton of Paignton.

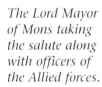

The Lord Mayor of Mons taking the salute along with officers of the Allied forces.

anchorage, where the Germans scuttled their ships. The German national situation became hopeless and, on 9 November, Kaiser Wilhelm abdicated and fled to his castle in Austria.

In France the guns of the warring nations fell silent. The Great War, called the war to end all wars, came to an end. German despondency and misery contrasted sharply with the relief and rejoicing felt by the victorious Allies.

In Belgium, which first bore the brunt and horror of German invasion in 1914, the City of Mons, on 15 November 1918, celebrated victory with a march past of British, French and American troops at the 'Grand Place' by Mons cathedral.

Many hundreds of families in Torbay lost loved ones during the years of war. This, and the economic depression that was to follow, changed the face of the nation forever.

THE BOOK OF TORBAY

THE LOST GENERATION

This photograph of a group of boys (above) *who played in the local cricket team was taken in a field off Marldon Hill, now an area covered with houses. The football group shown* (below) *was probably taken about 1910 or 1911, some three or four years before the Great War. It was photographed at Paignton's North Green and the trees in the background indicate the position of the hotels from Sattva to Bonair. Many of these boys fought in the Great War; several did not return and their names are on the war memorial in Palace Avenue. Those shown in the photographs include: Leonard Evans; Gerry Milton; Edgar Newcombe; Douglas and Gordon Foale; Rex and Leslie Axworthy; Howard Spry; Jack Robinson; Reg Letcher; Tom and Dick Adams; Percy Radford; Alec Philip; Gilbert Martin; Rex Rogers; Leslie Bultz; Percy Dammerell; B. Smardon; R. Williams; Arthur and Harold Came; Fred Stranger; E. Woodward and E. J. Bowerman.*

19 – Into the Roaring Twenties

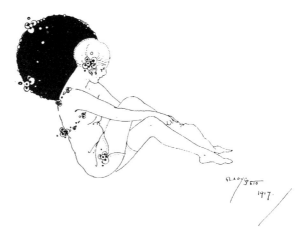

Following the end of hostilities, came demobilization. Those who had survived came home only to face a new peril. The whole world was plunged into the disaster of the Spanish Flu epidemic which killed millions – certainly more than perished in the four years of war. Nearly a quarter of a million people died in Britain alone. Despite its healthy position Torbay had its share of grief.

The joy of demobilization was also tempered by the fact that the returning heroes found that Britain was not the 'land fit for heroes' as Prime Minister Lloyd George had promised. There was massive unemployment. Heroes and non-heroes, colonels and corporals, admirals and able-seamen waited in the same dole queues for a government handout.

However, despite the 1920s and the 1930s being the periods of the Great Depression, those fortunate enough to have survived the war, set out to enjoy themselves. Women in particular embarked upon a wild social spree that gave to the era the description the 'Roaring Twenties'.

Gladys Peto's drawing reveals something of the naughtiness of the Roaring Twenties.

This was due in part to the loss of a whole generation of young marriageable men, and partly to the emancipation that women had found as a result of their work in the factories during the conflict.

What little money young women had was often spent on having fun: dancing the night away to the rhythm of the foxtrot, quickstep, Charleston and the black bottom, revelling in the new sound of the jazz bands. In Torquay, the Marine Spa ballroom throbbed and pulsated to the strident music rendered by the best and latest orchestras.

An afternoon 'tea dance' at the Marine Spa ballroom in the 1930s.

Crowds throng the street at Paignton's Shopping Week c.1920.

THE SPECIAL SHOPPING WEEKS

During the 1920s, Paignton Chamber of Commerce organised a yearly 'shopping week' with various competitions including window dressing and other attractions designed to stimulate trade. These were highly successful, as shown in the photograph of the crowds in Torbay Road. This was typical of other popular events such as the Annual Regatta, and the Carnival which drew large crowds to the seafront.

By 1919 women's fashions rapidly had changed. Hats were pulled well down over the brow, skirts were narrowed into what was known as the Tube Look. One wit of the period summed it up with these few lines:

With hat tipped over no eye free,
Tis very plain she cannot see,
With skirts so tight it causes talk,
Tis very plain she cannot walk,
And yet she misses tram cars, buses,
Never hurries, never fusses.
Man never could survive, poor chap,
With just one half that handicap.

Those who preferred not to dance, found consolation in the make-believe world of the silver screen. Cinemas in Torbay in the 1920s were showing such silent films as 'The Gold Rush' with Charlie Chaplin, 'Ben Hur', 'The Jazz Singer', and the first Laurel and Hardy film 'Big Business'. The Electric cinema at Brixham opened in 1935 with 'The 39 Steps' but before 1935 Brixham had a small cinema which had opened in 1905.

From the mid 1920s onward women became increasingly independent, self-assured, and within reason, did as they liked, behaved as they liked, flaunting the old traditions. In essence they rebelled, firmly dismantling deeply entrenched Victorianism. They wanted change, a break from the unrelenting boredom and labour of everyday routine. One path to freedom was the holiday break. And from the southern shores of the westcountry, Torbay, with its long coastline of beaches and coves, of sand and shingle, of blue skies and sunshine, beckoned seductively.

THE BOOK OF TORBAY

TRADERS ADVERTISING IN PAIGNTON REGATTA PROGRAMMES 1919-23

FRED SARSON	Pharmacist. Palace Avenue.
GILES & SON	Shoe Repairs. 24 Palace Avenue (later Wongs Chinese Restaurant).
CARR & QUICK	Wine Merchants. 60 Winner St.
J. BOND & SON	Furniture Dealers. Dartmouth Rd.
H. HUNTER & SON	Jeweller. 9 Victoria Street (later MacFisheries).
NORMAN BRAUND	Draper. Victoria Street (later Burlman).
A. J. HOLMAN	Clock House (later Eric Lloyd - the clock is still there.
EVANS & SONS	Bakers. 12 Weston Place (later Clarke, Furnishers).
H. C. LORIMER	Drapers. Victoria Street (later Dorothy Perkins).
H. M. LANGFORD	Leather Goods. 57 Torbay Road (later Porterhouse).
TORBAY MILL	Winner Street.
W. T MITCHELMORE	Jeweller. Palace Avenue.
S. BATTEN	Builder. 112 Winner Street (later Pets' Parlour)
COLINS & CLARK	Motor Engineers. Palace Avenue (the triangular block dividing Dartmouth Road and Totnes Road, originally the Liberal Club).
J. PERRETT	Hatter & Hosier. Torbay Road.
J. LIDSTONE	Watchmaker. 2 Dartmouth Road.
GOSS MABIN	Jeweller. 41 Torbay Rd.
R. POPE	Dairyman. Howard Terrace, Winner Street.
J. SUTTON	Stationer. 71 Torbay Road (later Mario's Ice Cream).
TREMEER'S	Bakers. 11 Palace Avenue.
H. GARDENER	Ironmonger. 49 Torbay Road (later Variety Fare).
J. H. GERMAN & SON	Photographer. Torbay Road
MORTIMER RICKS	Jeweller. Victoria Street.
SPRY & SONS	20 Victoria Street (later Alliance Building Society).
A. EVANS	Outfitters. (later demolished).
VICTORIA DRUG CO	Station Square (later Trant's tool shop).
E. BEARE	Draper. Victoria Street (later Liptons).

THE WALL STREET CRASH 1929

When at the close of the Great War in 1918, the Germans sailed their High Seas Fleet into Scapa Flow under the terms of surrender, it was thought that nation would never be able to launch another war as she had done three times before in 1814, 1870 and 1914. But hardly had the ink dried on the paper of the Peace Treaty than Germany began her preparations for a future war. This was made possible from the loans made by the United States and Great Britain to the vanquished foe, to the tune of £1500 million. By 1934 Germany had a military strength amounting to over one million men and 5000 aircraft. While by 1938 German factories were producing 1000 aircraft per month, the British Prime Minister Stanley Baldwin was proposing that Britain and France should each reduce their air forces to a total of 500 planes.

By 1929 the financial state of world markets appeared to be increasingly stable but a sudden and violent financial storm swept over the Wall Street Stock Exchange to develop into what became known as the Wall Street Crash. The prosperity of millions of American homes had been built on a gigantic structure of inflated credit, all without substance.

Twenty thousand banks suspended payment and in the wake of the collapse, factories closed and unemployment in the USA rose to over ten million. Shares nose-dived to an unprecedented level and there was a stampede to sell everything for cash. Millions of small investors were made bankrupt overnight and many businessmen committed suicide.

The United States stock exchange was buried under a flood of liquidation which soon surged not only against the tranquil shores of Britain but on the mainlands of European and Eastern states creating worldwide recession. The effect in Britain was disastrous. Factories and shipyards closed, throwing thousands on the dole; the payment of which was woefully inadequate. A married man with two children received only 29 shillings per week, barely subsistence level. Unemployment rose to three million.

Ironically, the song that hit the music world just prior to the crash was 'Happy Days Are Here Again'!

The 1930 economic meltdown made its presence felt well into the mid thirties, particularly effecting holiday resorts like Torbay. Some hotels were forced into bankruptcy or became heavily mortgaged, ownership passing to the banks. Proprietors of guest houses and small hotels who had spent their meagre savings in property improvement to keep pace with the former flourishing holiday trade, suddenly found themselves without summer bookings and the normal deposits on which they depended to pay winter bills.

In Devon generally, small, formerly prosperous businesses had no alternative but to close, forcing hundreds to join the dole queues. In some of Torbay's poorer areas, several households with large families faced starvation. There were occasions when bakers and foodshops gave handouts, and charitable institutions made food contributions. Undoubtedly, the early thirties were the bad times but thankfully they passed, to usher in a new period of prosperity. Businesses re-opened, new building projects appeared, the holiday trade picked up, unemployment figures dropped and the visitors returned. With a few shillings in their pockets and some cheer in their hearts, the people of Torbay flocked to the cinemas to see such movies as 'Snow White and the Seven Dwarfs', 'King Kong', 'Cleopatra' and the screen's favourite, Judy Garland in 'Over the Rainbow'.

20 – The Thirties and Beyond

The thirties saw the resorts of Torquay, Paignton and Brixham take on something of the character that was to typify English holiday resorts over the coming decades. Cheap public transport, longer holidays for the working classes, and the promotion of holidays through advertisements, added to Torbay's special status as one of the country's most select holiday destinations. The photographs on the following pages reveal the exciting atmosphere of this period in Torbay's past.

Abbey Sands and Café. The Collonade Shelter was built in 1928; this photograph is c.1930.

Paignton Green in the 1930s showing the peir and the little bandstand.

87

A small part of Goodrington Sands taken around the late twenties–early thirties, before the clifftop became dominated by three large hotels.

Above: *Trams and taxis compete for passengers in this view of a sunny morning on The Strand in 1930. The tram, right centre, is passing Timothy White's the 'Cash Chemists'.*

Right: *Crowds on Torre Abbey Sands c.1935.*

Paignton seafront gardens in the 1930s. The Festival Hall was later built on this site.

Carnival procession at Torquay seafront, 1932

The Drum Inn at Cockington, a favourite spot for tourists to Torbay. It was designed by Edward Lutyens in 1934 and was intended to be part of a much larger scheme for a model village centre. Eventually only the Inn was constructed in the style of a traditional village pub.

With the closing down of the tram service in 1934, Stentiford's newsagent shop which stood at the corner of Hyde Road and Torquay Road was knocked down and reconstructed about 15 feet to the right. At that time there were no shops to the left of Torquay Road. The objects against the sky are part of the electric tram overhead cable system. The London magazine Tatler *is advertised in the window at the right of the picture.*

The official opening of the cliff railway to Oddicombe Beach by Alderman Taylor, Mayor of Torquay, April 1926.

A NEW FESTIVAL HALL

On 2 February 1937, a joint meeting of the Paignton Chamber of Commerce and the Hotels and Boarding Houses Association was held at Evans Café (then in Torbay Road) to consider the possibility of an alternative building to the Public Hall (now called the Palace Avenue Theatre). There was much difference of opinion as to where a suitable building for conferences and stage shows should be sited and the estimated cost of £30 000 was a substantial delaying factor, so Paignton had to wait another thirty years before the Festival Hall was built.

The Hotels and Boarding Association original logo, designed by Sutton Printers who were founder members of the association along with the Secretary Miss Lavers and the Treasurer Mrs Parkinson.

1930S BRIXHAM

Early morning at Brixham's Fish Market in the 1930s.

Brixham's Fore Street in the early 1930s. Horse-drawn transport was growing less common as motor transport increased. On the left is the Co-operative Society store whose delivery van is parked across the road.

21 – The Torquay Flood

On the 3 and 4 August 1938, Torquay suffered its worst storm flood in living memory. In that twenty-four hour period 6.4 inches of rain fell on the town, causing havoc to many private and business premises. Flanked by steep hills serving as conduits, water poured down into the basin of the town on through Castle Circus to lower Fleet Street.

One of the worst affected areas was where the watercourse from St Marychurch raced down Chatto Road into Lymington Road flooding the terrace houses there to a depth of some eight feet. Surging on, the flow was increased by the torrent racing down from Upton Hill, onward in to Castle Circus, there joined by the waters coursing down St Marychurch Road, Tor Church Road and Higher Union Street.

Here heavy manhole covers were torn away allowing trapped underground water to spout high into the air. By this time the racing flow had developed into a torrent sweeping on into Fleet Street where in its onward rush it had formed a junction with the flow from Market Street. In Fleet Street the ground floor of the large Rockhey premises and those either side, were overwhelmed by the force which swept through, destroying valuable stock. Before finally expending its power and violence by gushing over the harbour walls at the Strand, it raced on into Abbey Place at the lower end of Swan Street burst open the doors of the business premises of Slades Grocers flooding the shop to a depth of around five feet.

Some goods were salvaged the next day by boats rowing into the shop and recovering undamaged goods from the higher shelves. One of the highlights of that eventful morning of the 4 August was when a certain bank manager was seen crossing Fleet Street in his bathing costume trying to reach the bank, with the keys firmly attached to a chain around his waist. Perhaps he wanted to check liquid assets. Brixham and Paignton were also affected by the storm but to a lesser degree according to damage reports. Below is a photograph of the flooded streets in Brixham.

A bus struggles through the floodwaters in Brixham, August 1938.

Part of the historical tableaux at Paignton's Church Street Fair, 1941. Sir Walter Raleigh (Mr W. Hodge) spreads his cloak to allow Queen Elizabeth (Mrs E. Western) to walk across the famous puddle.

Right: *'Arise Sir Francis...'. Queen Elizabeth knights England's sea-faring hero Sir Francis Drake (Mr W. Western).*

Below: *Crowds watch the Flora Dance being performed through Church Street, Paignton, 1941.*

22 – Paignton's Church Street Fair, 1941

Church Street Fair centred around the Parish Church of St John the Baptist. It was a very important event in the town's activities, with local residents and shopkeepers wholeheartedly contributing to make it a success.

Bands, dancing, stalls, games and competitions brought large crowds to Church Street to join in the fun of the fair. The period costumes worn and made by a legion of helpers who worked night after night producing Elizabethan garments provided a pageantry of colour to the whole event. The Parish Church garden with its panoply of floral hues afforded an agreeable and natural backdrop to the tableaux of ancient heraldry and the enactments of scenes from Tudor days.

The whole purpose of the occasion was to raise money for the local hospital which overlooked the fair from its vantage point. Some of the entertainment was also centred around Church Street's Crown and Anchor Way, which now provides a traffic short-cut into Palace Avenue.

Historically, Crown and Anchor Way played an important part in the town's business as far back as the early 1800s. In those days it was a staging post for the stagecoach which would drive through the old archway to the rear yard and there change tired horses for fresh ones. When the days of the stagecoach ended, the yard became a slaughterhouse.

Even as late as 1930, herds of sheep and cattle were driven along nearby Well Street, in through the arch to the yard beyond, there to be slaughtered, their carcases hung along the walls to await collection.

Some of the entrants for the costume parade held in the Parish Church grounds are (left to right): Paddy Hooper, Audrey Hooper, Betty Bond, Joan Hooper, Joan Western, Gwen Craze and Lucy Hooper.

Western's Bakery and Confectionary premises in Church Street with Mr and Mrs Western and daughter Joan dressed in period costume prior to the Fair's Dress Parade. This was in 1941, hence the splinter binding on the windows as a precaution against possible bomb blast.

In the late 1930s few suspected that the country was about to be plunged into war and life in the resort went on much as before. Here summer crowds enjoy the Promenade sunshine to the accompaniment of a military band. Inset: Sheet music from popular songs of the day and a seaside cartoon by G.E. Studdy.

23 – The Clouds of War

Although between 1933 and 1939, Europe was ridden with the opposing factions of Fascism and Communism, and in constant contention, the British people shrugged it off as of no concern of theirs. This period of European unrest seemed to have transferred some of its burdens to the English throne for 1936 became known as the 'year of the three kings', a year of extraordinary crisis.

George V died in January and was succeeded by his son Edward, Prince of Wales. Against the wishes of the Government his mother, Queen Mary, and a large proportion of the British people, Edward proposed to marry a divorced American woman Mrs Wallis Simpson. If he did so, it would mean that by his ascension to the throne, Mrs Simpson would become Queen. In line with the terms of the constitution, the Government and the Commonwealth refused to allow this. Edward could either have the Crown or Mrs Simpson. He chose Mrs Simpson and abdicated. This led to the Coronation of his brother George VI in May 1937.

But during this period, the clouds of war were gathering apace and the power of Fascism growing. And while the heads of the nations argued about other things, there strode upon the world stage Adolf Hitler, the Dictator of Germany, who was to prove himself a Satanic genius. His was a dictatorship based on rule by terror, reeking with blood, which eventually accounted for the extermination of 60 million people in the war that would erupt in 1939.

In London in 1936, Hitler's fellow fascist, Sir Oswald Mosley, led a rally of some 7000 Blackshirted Fascists in Trafalgar Square, where his hooligan bodyguards brandished the Swastika, beating up those who interrupted Mosley's militant oratory, leaving a trail of over 100 badly injured.

These events in London at that time held no particular interest for the people of Devon, that is until Mosley himself, along with his bloodthirsty cohorts arrived in Torquay, preaching the gospel of anarchy and violence. The author recalls this disciple of Adolf Hitler with his hoodlums staging a demonstration in Albert Road, Torquay, behind Market Street (where now stands the Haldon

The coronation of King George VI

Shopping Centre). Anyone who voiced opposition was pounced upon by Mosley's men and beaten up. Why Mosley ever thought he could convert the the people of Torquay to Fascism, especially by these Draconian measures remains a mystery, but there is no doubt this poisonous rhetoric left a lasting and odious impression on all those who were present. However it was to be only four years later that Hitler's bombs fell on the towns of Torbay, the foetid finger of the Swastika tarnishing this golden Queen of the Devon coast.

In those pre-war years, the resorts of Torquay, Paignton and Brixham were packed with visitors determined to enjoy themselves. The famous bands of Ted Heath, Victor Sylvester, Ron Goodwin and Ivy Benson's all-Women's Band at the Marine Spa kept the crowds dancing far into the night. During the day, on the promenade., holidaymakers lounged in deck-chairs listening to the Torquay Military Band; it was an idyllic way to spend a morning or afternoon in the warm sunshine.

In July 1939, just before the outbreak of the Second World War, units of the German Fleet

THE BOOK OF TORBAY

In the late 1930s the German Foreign Minister negotiated a number of treaties with European countries which he knew Germany would not honour. His visit to Torquay in 1939 was undoubtedly part of a mission to discover the depth of sympathy for the Nazi cause in Britain.

arrived in Torbay on a goodwill visit. For such an occasion several well known Nazi personalities were present, including Hitler's Foreign Minister Herr Joachim von Ribbentrop, whom the author met momentarily at the Marine Spa. Also present was the German Ambassador Dr Herbert von Dirksen. The presence of Ribbentrop in the Spa ballroom was apparently something of a secret for no reporters were present.

The visit of such important men was of interest, especially at such a critical and sensitive period when Germany and Britain were on the verge of war. Among the visitors would have been Grand Admiral Erich Raeder, Commander-in-Chief of the German navy, with some of his principal ships. The arrival of the fleet was an opportunity to show off some of their best ships like the battlecruisers *Gneisenau* and *Scharnhorst*.

As the storm clouds grew darker and war seemed inevitable, holiday makers and residents in the resorts became doggedly determined to make the most of their peacetime freedom while they could. There was an underlying impression that this August Bank Holiday would be the last before the impact of a world conflict would disrupt their ordered lives. And so, they set out to enjoy themselves, with coach tours, river trips, picnics on the beaches and moors, attending carnivals, fetes, and sporting events. Theatre shows attracted many, as did dancing to the latest hit 'The Chestnut Tree' and listening to the dulcet tones of Vera Lynn singing 'Yours'. Elderly couples enjoyed dancing to the slower rhythm of 'The Anniversary Waltz'.

The highlight in July was a visit by the King and Queen and the Royal Princesses Elizabeth and Margaret to Dartmouth. They arrived aboard the Royal Yacht, *Victoria & Albert,* and came ashore to drive to the Britannia Royal Naval College along the embankment lined with thousands of people.

In Torquay, there were excellent shows running at theatres and the Pavilion boasted stars such as Evelyn Laye, Robb Wilton, Donald Pears and many more. Also for a while, the Midland's Broadcasting dance band, under the direction of Billy Gammon, played popular music at the Spa ballroom every evening to crowds of dancers enjoying 'In the still of the Night' and George Elricks 'Nursie, Nursie'. At cinemas, crowds queued to see such films as 'Robin Hood' and Charlie Chaplin's 'The Great Dictator.'

The news that everyone had been dreading, came on that Sunday morning 3 September, when the Prime Minister, Neville Chamberlain, broadcast to the nation, closing his announcement with the words 'therefore this country is now at war with Germany'.

All Chamberlain's previous assurances that there would be no war, all his misplaced resistance to re-armament, all his declarations of 'peace in our time' were shattered. Having gambled all on his policy of conciliation and lost, Chamberlain, a broken man could only stare into the ruin that lay around him. The man who stepped forward to take his place was Winston Churchill.

And so, Britain went to war naked and vulnerable, facing with courage and resolution, the seemingly impossible task ahead. Yet despite the dark days that loomed, it was Winston Churchill's clarion calls to the nation that lifted morale, raised hope and nurtured determination to fight back until final victory was won: 'We shall fight on the landing grounds, we shall fight in the fields and in the streets, we shall fight in the hills, we shall never surrender.'

Thus despite the gravity of the European situation, Torbay businesses tried to carry on in a normal way. Restaurants and cafes were doing very well. At the Tudor Rose on Vaughan Parade,

A rare photograph taken from a neighbouring ship showing HMS Courageous *listing heavily following the torpedo strikes from a German U boat on 17 September 1939.*

Torquay, a delectable afternoon cream tea cost two shilling and sixpence, while the Torquay-to-Guernsey passenger trip was sixteen shillings. At Evans Outfitters in Church Street Paignton, one could buy a Gent's suit, ready to wear for £2, and Brocks Furnishers in Victoria Street were offering Oak Bedroom suites from £15.

Meanwhile Torquay Council were concerned about the slow progress on seafront improvements, the erosion of Babbacombe cliff, and the arrangements for the reception of evacuees from London and elsewhere.

It was at this time that the Imperial Hotel received notification from the Ministry of Defence that the hotel was to be requisitioned for use as a hospital. The news came as a bombshell for the hotel was full with guests. Within hours, notices of evacuation had been issued to all the guests, food orders cancelled and every member of the staff given notice of termination of employment. By the 6 October the hotel was an empty shell with no furniture, no staff, and no manager. Then without any explanation the Ministry's requisition was withdrawn.

Instant action and vital decisions had to be made. Some sort of restoration was accomplished with a skeleton staff and a new manager, Michael Chapman, who in this capacity and later as Managing Director, over the next 45 years not only maintained the hotel's prestigious reputation but enhanced its reputation both nationally and internationally.

Meanwhile, during that early war period, in October 1939, there were clear signs that preparations for war were already well in hand by the many appeals from the ARP (Air Raid Precautions) and the Home Guard.

Only two weeks after the declaration of war, on 17 September, the first impact of the horror of the conflict reached Torbay. This was the news that the Plymouth-based aircraft carrier HMS *Courageous* had been torpedoed by a U boat (U29) and sunk only 300 miles from Lands End, with the loss of over 500 of her crew. Some of whom the crew were Torbay men and local survivors gave horrifying accounts of why so many had died from exposure in the sea. Because of Britain's state of unreadiness, ships were rushed to sea, many carrying crews of untrained young conscripts and elderly Royal Naval Reserve Pensioners. Unwisely deployed on anti-submarine patrol in the Western Approaches, *Courageous* sank with heavy loss of life, caused mainly by ineffective life-saving equipment.

Kapitan-Leutnant Otto Schubert, commander of U boat U.29 is congratulated by the German Grand Admiral Karl Dönitz following the sinking of HMS Courageous.

It appears that during the twenty-one years peace period between 1918 and 1939, the Carley float life-saving rafts fastened to the side of the ship had been painted over with thick paint every year without being moved. As the ship was sinking the 1200 crew rushed to the floats but these were stuck to the side of the ship, immoveable. It was because of this and the fact that *Courageous* had been rushed to sea without lifebelts being issued, that over 500 men needlessly died. With the sinking of *Courageous*, the war at sea had begun in earnest.

In Torbay, during the last days of that peaceful balmy summer of 1939, people braced themselves for whatever was to come. ARP drills were increased and 69 000 gas masks checked and prepared ready for distribution. In the event of invasion from the sky or sea, the Ministry of Information and the War Office issued the order 'What To Do If the Invador Comes':

Issued by the Ministry of Information in co-operation with the War Office and the Ministry of Home Security.

If the
INVADER
comes

WHAT TO DO — AND HOW TO DO IT

A few extracts from the instruction leaflet (above) to the civilian population issued in 1940 and 1941 :

... If the Germans come by parachute, aeroplane or ship, you must remain where you are. The order is "stay put." If you run away you will be exposed to far greater danger because you will be machine gunned from the air ...

... Be calm, quick and exact, keep watch. If you see anything suspicious note it carefully and go at once to nearest police or military office ...

... Do not give any German anything, do not tell him anything. Hide your food and your bicycle, hide your maps, see that the enemy gets no petrol. If you have a car or a motorbicycle put it out of action when not in use ...

24 – Torbay's Home Front

There is no doubt that Hitler had every intention to launch a massive invasion of England at the earliest possible moment. This extract from his diary dated 31 July 1940 is clear evidence:

The decisive result can only be achieved by an attack on England. An attempt must therefore be made to prepare the operation for 15th September 1940. The decision as to whether the operation is to take place in September or is to be delayed until May 1941 will be made after the Air Force has made concentrated attacks on Southern England after one week.

Following the evacuation of the British Army from Dunkirk in May 1940, the danger of a German invasion was real enough. Apart from the remnants of the evacuated forces, the country rallied a voluntary army of civilians, called the Local Defence Volunteers (later known as the Home Guard) to defend our coastline. In retrospect, we can now see how frighteningly ineffectual this and our gun battery defence was at the time. At first the Home Guard was poorly armed: when rifles were unobtainable, there appeared on parade shotguns, sporting rifles and perhaps a pistol or two. Where no firearms were available, the pike or pitchfork was carried.

When Herr von Ribbentrop visited Rome in 1940, he was reported as saying to Count Ciano, Mussolini's son-in-law 'The English territorial defence system is non-existent. A single German Division will bring complete collapse.'

Although Churchill always admired the courage and resolution of the Home Guard he often wondered what would have happened if two hundred thousand German storm troopers had arrived on the shores of the English coastline.

Members of Torquay's Local Defence Volunteers guarding Greathill Reservoir in 1940. Their weaponry would have given them little chance against German troops but there is little doubt that these men would have fought bravely against any invaders.

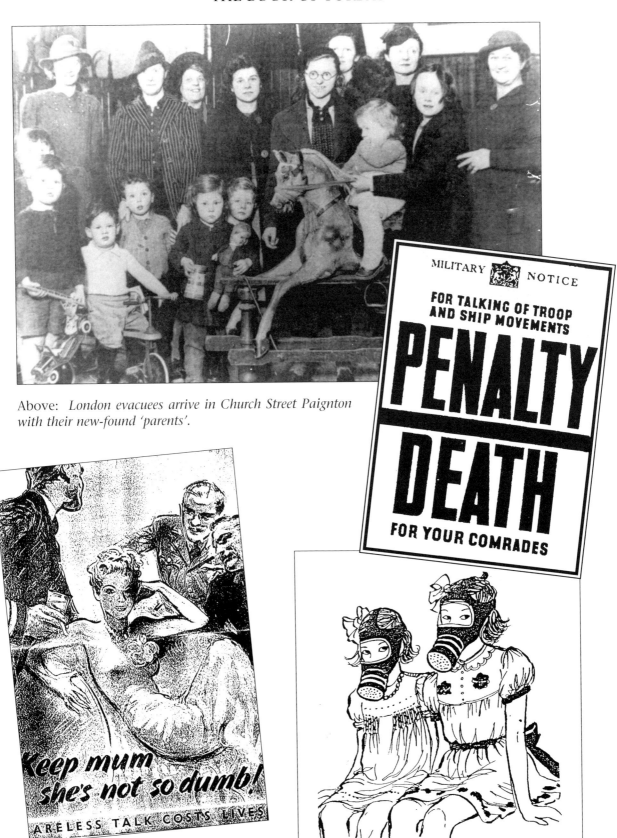

Above: *London evacuees arrive in Church Street Paignton with their new-found 'parents'.*

Wartime information and propaganda was widely circulated. These posters warn of the dangers of spies gaining important information from casual conversation - and its consequences. On the outbreak of war in 1939, gas masks were issued to all civilians, including babies.

Wartime food parcels arrive from South Africa for the retired fishermen of Brixham.

As pressing as the fear of attack from the air and in Torbay, as elsewhere, local ironmongers began stocking their stores with steel shelters. Many residents dug deep holes in their gardens in order to create their own style of air raid shelter.

In the face of these chilling reminders about the possibility of invasion and attack, most found some consolation in the latest songs of the time. One of the catchy tunes was 'The Lambeth Walk' from Lupino Lane's London production of 'Me and My Girl', another was 'Bella Bambina'.

Wartime entertainment was carried by the BBC and radio was to play a major part in the propaganda war. Billy Cotton's band broadcast Noel Gay's 'Run Rabbit Run' and many other shows were deliberately intended to boost civilian morale. Many will recall the haunting melody sung by Gracie Fields 'Wish Me Luck As You Wave Me Goodbye' from the film version of 'Shipyard Sally.'

Especially in the early period of the war, when Britain stood alone against the German offensive, parcels and gifts arrived for the beleagured Britons from many parts of the Commonwealth, and from the USA. From South Africa came food parcels for Brixham's retired fishermen. The gifts of tinned meat, jellies, sweets and canned fruit meant a great deal to people whose diet was seriously affected by rationing. Some of these parcels were distributed by the Chairman of the Urban District Council, Mr J. Heron who asked Lt-Colonel R.W.Johnson, the Food Executive Officer for Brixham, to convey heartfelt thanks to their unknown friends in South Africa.

In the Battle of the Atlantic during 1942, the tide of war was flowing in favour of the enemy. The mission for German warships and U boats was to destroy supplies to Britain and thereby force her into surrender. In one period of eight months, a staggering two million tons of British shipping and hundreds of lives were lost. But as the war moved towards 1943, there came a rising tide of confidence and optimism in the country. Shortly before the beginning of 1942 Japan had attacked Pearl Harbor, bringing the USA into the war on Britain's side. The news lifted British spirits to new levels. One day, not far distant, American troops would land on British shores to carry the battle to the enemy and to victory.

THE BOOK OF TORBAY

The Air Raid Precautions (ARP) units were among the most vital of all those who fought the war on the Home Front. The picture above shows wardens of the post near Lammas Lane, Paignton. They are photographed complete with stirrup pumps, rattles and bells. The warden with the large gloves, seated on the right, was Mr Frank Martin, who had a furniture shop in Torquay Road and was later a Mayor of Torbay.

Air raid wardens for the Preston area c. 1940

25 – Bombs Over the Bay

In May 1943, Hitler ordered his bomber planes to attack random targets with tip-and-run raids along the south coast of England. Although the resort of Torquay had no major military installations, it was well known as a base for recuperating soldiers, with one of the region's largest hospitals for officers at the former Palace Hotel.

On Sunday 30 May 1943, at Caen-Carpiquet in Northern France, twenty-one single seater Focke-Wulf 190s, loaded with 1000lb high explosive bombs took off from the airfield heading northwest, their target the holiday resort of Torquay, 160 miles distant. Flying at 240 miles miles per hour, at barely 50 feet above the channel waves to avoid detection from British radar, only forty minutes later, at 2.30pm, defence units at Hope's Nose spotted the enemy planes and activated the warning sirens at Torquay and Brixham.

It was a bright sunny day with people relaxing on Torquay seafront enjoying the warm sunshine. Then from across the bay came a low whisper merging into a rhythmic hum like a swarm of angry bees, the familiar drone of the dreaded Focke-Wulf bomber. They appeared as little dots at first, growing larger every moment, the pilots carefully plotting their course by the siting of Thatcher Rock and Hopes Nose. They then rose sufficiently to clear the higher structures along the coastline, speeding onwards in a deafening roar.

At the Parish church of St Marychurch that afternoon a special children's service had been arranged and the church was filled with children and parents. The bombers raced on, bomb doors open, their fire-spitting cannons indiscriminately dispensing death and destruction.

Inside the building the congregation heard the wail of the sirens and just at that moment cannon shells from the approaching aircraft struck the building. Almost simultaneously a 1000lb bomb tore away the church roof like paper to land within the confines of the walls. There it exploded among the mixed assembly of children and adults. The result was a nightmare, the world of hallowed peace and sanctity suddenly erupting in an earthquake of disintegration, blinding the senses, hurling bodies and stone and timber in all directions.

Walls were ripped away like cardboard, massive stone arches hurled aside, while the roof, now unsupported, collapsed on the carnage below.

As the aircraft wheeled away over the town a pall of dust and smoke rose from the church like a funeral pyre and from its centre came the cries and screams of those still alive.

There is no direct evidence to suggest that the church was the target but it is interesting to note that altogether seven bombs, one each from seven pilots, were dropped on or around the church. Certainly the raid was brief, cruel, and horrific. In those death-dealing ten seconds, 45 people were killed outright including 23 children. Another 157 were injured.

In the resort a total of 330 houses were either damaged or demolished during the raid. But the Luftwaffe also paid a heavy price for the attack. Torquay's ant-aircraft defences had been greatly strengthened in the previous few weeks and were fully armed, ready and waiting.

As the bombers dived on to their target they were met by a wall of flak from the combined firepower of the 4-inch Bofors anti-aircraft guns, and

Focke-Wulf 190 of the type that attacked Torbay on 30 May 1943

Vicker's machine-guns. Hardly had the strident wail of the warning sirens died, than the Focke-Wulf 190s were upon them, the air filled with a cacophony of battle noise the roar of racing engines rising to a crescendo, the flash and crash of exploding shells and cannon fire and the vicious thud and crump of bursting bombs.

The pilot of the plane responsible for the dropping of the 1000lb bomb that plunged into the Parish church, paid the extreme penalty. His aircraft rent and burning, engines roaring, weaving and banking in an effort to escape, was suddenly confronted by the spire of the nearby Roman Catholic church of Our Lady and St Denis. Frantically trying to avoid a collision he banked up steeply to the left but too late. In a sickening lurch, the tip of the port wing struck the upper spire of the church and clawed the aircraft around, forcing it to head inland.

Rapidly losing height and now out of control it crashed on to a house in Teignmouth Road where it burst into flame, killing the pilot and causing severe burns to a young woman.

It had been Torquay's most tragic raid but, ironically, this was also the last attack on the resort in 1943. Perhaps this was due to the loss of six out

Rescuers clearing debris at the parish church in St Marychurch following the air raid of 30 May 1943 in which 45 people were killed.

of the twenty-one aircraft inflicted by the efficiency of the anti-aircraft defence force. Torquay was free of raids for exactly one year until the 29 May 1944, when enemy aircraft attacked over the bay, particularly the Harbour district, where landing barges were moored ready for D-Day, the 6 June 1944.

Frequent bombing raids were made on the towns of Torquay, Paignton and Brixham during the war resulting in many casualties and much damage. Although the towns of Torbay suffered much less than the neighbouring towns of Plymouth and Exeter with their massive 'blitzes', the following figures issued by the Civil Defence Organisation up to October 1944, reflect the seriousness of the Torbay attacks: 168 killed and nearly 500 injured, and 137 houses destroyed and nearly 14 000 damaged.

Left and below: *Workers clearing up the interior of the church in the days following the raid at St Marychurch*

THE MILITARY HOSPITAL

The ruins of the former Palace Hotel, Torquay, used as a wartime military hospital, following the air raid attack in October 1942.

Among Torquay's many responsibilities was its important role as a military hospital base for British and Commonwealth, Polish and Free French wounded soldiers who had fought alongside British troops. Men from most of the Allied nations who could be seen on Torquay seafront dressed in blue hospital uniform, struggling to recover from wounds and shellshock, legacies of the battlefronts of North Africa and Italy. Many who came to Torquay to recuperate did not survive the German bombing and strafing to which the town was constantly subjected. Even the Palace Hotel, one of the main military hospitals, clearly marked with a large Red Cross on its rooftop was heavily bombed and partially destroyed.

26 – The Yanks are Coming

US troops march past Brixham Town Hall, 1943.

In mid January 1944, people in the Castle Circus area were aware of the sound of marching feet. Here they saw thousands of soldiers, line abreast, stretching as far as the eye could see, marching towards the Lymington Road parks. The excited cry of 'They're Americans' spread like wildfire. They had never seen US troops before. Later it was rumoured that 30 000 had arrived in the area. There was an immediate sense of relief. A feeling that with American support the war would be brought to a speedy end.

Billeting had of course been arranged in advance and soon nearly every hotel, guest house or private household had Americans under their roof, packed into accommodation like sardines. Although most were billeted, one Company was housed in Nissen huts behind the Regent Cinema (now the bus station). They called the sea 'the ocean', drawing pins were 'thumb tacks', the pavement, 'the sidewalk' and Mr Garth had to put out a sign that he was a 'barber' as they did not recognise 'hairdresser'.

The US Engineers turned the Old Brixham Road from a lane into a wide road to allow the passage of tanks and lorries, and built a new slipway in Torquay Harbour ready for the invasion of Normandy. The GIs were extremely generous, had plenty of food and spent their money freely.

Often there were absences from billets while they were sent on battle exercises to Slapton Sands. Some never returned, following the terrible tregedy there in April 1944 when German E Boats sank several landing craft during night practice landings.

D-Day was the best kept secret of all time. It remains a miracle how the Germans were kept in the dark about the largest invasion in history until it was too late, and Allied troops and armour poured into Normandy's beaches with overwhelming force. More than two years of meticulous planning, conspired to throw Hitler's war machine off balance and seal the success of Operation Overlord. The element of surprise was the single most potent weapon in wrong-footing

A newspaper story from 1943: Carol Littlewood, an evacuee from North London, attempts to dodge the restrictions but US Military Police maintain their 'keep out' policy.

the Nazis and dislodging them from Fortress Europe.

If the Allies won, they would sow the seeds of a new future; if they lost, Hitler's reign of terror and torture would take over the whole world. Seven thousand ships were waiting, loaded with troops ready to go. Eleven thousand planes were standing by, with eighteen thousand paratroopers and thousands of gliders. In ports all along the southern coast of England 200 000 assault troops were crammed into landing craft.

As the people of the United Kingdom, United States, Canada and many other countries switched on their wireless sets on the morning of the 6 June,1944, they heard the following announcement on the news bulletin:

This morning under the command of General Dwight D. Eisenhower, naval forces, supported by strong air forces, began landing Allied armies on the northern coast of France.

It was an announcement which brought mixed feelings: excitement tempered with composure, gladness tinged with anxiety, hope moderated with caution.

Across the channel, while the beaches of Normandy erupted into a hellish inferno of flame and shell, and Allied soldiers fought and died in their hundreds. In Torbay, as elsewhere, parents were in a torment of anxiety about the safety of their loved ones on the beaches of Normandy.

American serviceman pose for a souvenir photograph at Young's Park, Goodrington, Paignton c.1943.

During the time the Americans had been billeted here, strong bonds of friendship had been forged between them and the people of Torquay, Paignton and Brixham. For them also many prayers were said for their survival.

After a long and bitter struggle Germany and her armies capitulated. Unconditional surrender came on the 7 May followed by VE-Day on 8 May. Although the war in the East was to continue for several months, the people expressed their relief in a tumultuous outburst of rejoicing. Torbay was alive with street parties; bunting and flags decorated every home, and womenfolk waited for their men to come home at last.

Top: *American troops march along The Strand, Torquay, ready to begin the embarkation for the D-Day landings.* Below: *Motor Torpedo Boats moored alongside Brixham breakwater, 1944.*

THE BOOK OF TORBAY

TORBAY AT WAR

The date is 3 June 1943, three days before the troops left for Normandy. This is the scene at Brixham hard, tanks and LTCs (landing craft - tank) are being loaded with supplies.

A US armoured unit aboard a landing craft.

27 – Celebrations

The end of the war was the signal for the greatest outburst of joy in the history of the victorious nations, even the vanquished felt some relief. But for the people of Britain, who in the early years had fought alone, there was a particular reason for celebration. Weary and worn, undaunted and triumphant, we had a moment that was ours, sublime. After nearly six years of tribulation, in which our towns and cities had been bombed into rubble, 65 000 civilians killed, endless nights, over many months, huddled in damp, cold bomb shelters, while thousands of tons of bombs rained down upon us, after all that, the people rejoiced. Never before or since, has such a spirit of unity and happiness existed.

All over Britain, and Torbay was no exception, there were parties and dancing in the open air. Long tables were laid end-to-end in the streets, with people gladly giving up the few rations they had to provide a feast. Decorations and flags fluttered gaily in the breeze.

On Paignton's seafront long lines of tables laden with food formed the centre point of their celebrations. In the town itself many people organised their own street parties while, in the evening, on Paignton Green, thousands gathered to enjoy open air dancing.

It was indeed a time of great happiness, but while the war may have been 'all over' in Europe, there was still a long way to go before the defeat of the Japanese in the Pacific. By August 1945, the United States, with the co-operation of their Allies, and in a bid to bring the Second World War to a final and quick solution, dropped an atomic bomb on the city of Hiroshima and another on Nagasaki forcing the Japanese to surrender. This brought an end to hostilities and 15 August was declared V.J. Day (Victory in Japan). It was the signal for another burst of rejoicing and more celebrations. Once again the streets echoed to the sound of music and dancing, a natural feeling of relief and an eagerness to build a new future.

The Mayor of Torquay, A. Denys Phillips, taking the salute at the march past on Torquay Strand during 'Salute the Soldier Week'.

Flight-Lt A. G. Ellis leads 1528 Squadron ATC in a Victory Parade to All Saints Church, Babbacombe, on 15 August 1945. The 1528 Squadron band played the whole parade past the Mayor of Torquay at the saluting base near the Norcliffe Hotel on Babbacombe Downs. Ellis was the author of a famous local history book and a history teacher at Torquay Grammar School.

The celebrations of victory in Torquay were mainly of thanksgiving. There was of course plenty of fun but the outstanding feature of the occasion was the seemly behaviour of everybody. Unfortunately, the authorities felt unable to release the coastal districts from the obligation of the black-out and so the night celebrations were devoid of the blaze of light which signalled victory in many other districts. At the Marine Spa, however, they put on the floodlighting for a few minutes immediately before the black-out time.

An afternoon service at the Torquay Pavilion, was arranged for 3pm on the day of the declaration of peace. But when it was stated that Winston Churchill was to make his speech at the very hour selected for the service it looked as though this might upset the programme. Cancellation of the arranged schedule of 'our' victory was unthinkable and the problem was solved by broadcasting the speech to the Pavilion congregation.

Well before the appointed hour the inhabitants began to assemble. It was an amazing gathering. No seats were reserved for anybody. As they came so they sat down together. It was a real get-together of the community. There were splashes of colour here and there where uniformed worshippers sat, singly or in pairs. Married couples or sweethearts in the services, khaki and blue, old and young, rich and poor. In front of the platform was the Municipal Orchestra and, behind, tier upon tier of a great choir.

Long before the hour, the doors had to be closed because the building was already very much overcrowded. Those unable to get in were quite upset and the Borough Treasurer, Mr E.C. Riding, did a great thing when he produced a portable wireless set and broadcast the Premier's speech to those shut out of the building. At exactly 3pm the sonorous tones of Big Ben boomed out the hour. A slight pause and then the voice of Winston Churchill was heard over the airwaves. There was no sound to interrupt the broadcast until he referred to the liberation of 'our dear Channel Islands' which so moved the audience that they broke into applause.

Following the broadcast the service continued. The great congregation lifted up its voice sincerely and heartily and emotion grew as the service moved to its conclusion.

Nearly every association and institution in Torbay did something to mark the occasion. At the Marine Spa there were special dance occasions each night with highly coloured decorations. Such was the hatred of the swastika after the five years of suffering that a Nazi flag was laid at the entrance to the Spa and used as a doormat. The Mayor and Mayoress of Torquay (Mr and Mrs A.

THE BOOK OF TORBAY

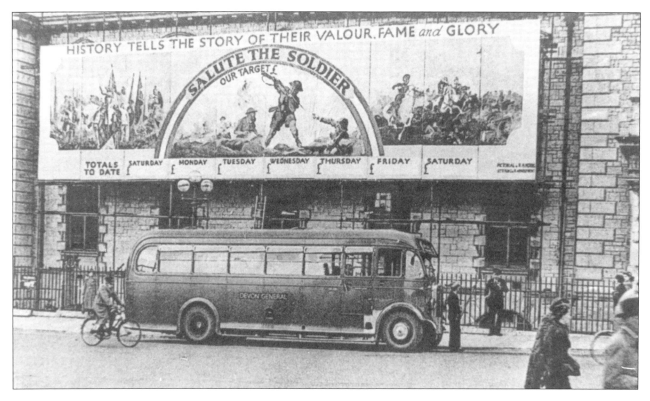

Torquay Town Hall displays a tribute to 'Salute the Soldier Week'. Centre is an AEC Regal single-decker bus on the Babbacombe and Watcombe run.

Advestisements from local newspapers reflect the relaxed times of post-war Torbay. Food and drink and dancing was back on the bill, and fashionable clothing was once again available in the shops.

115

Victory celebration in Paignton, 8 May 1945. Crowds gather to hear Winston Churchill's announcement read out in front of the public hall, now the Palace Avenue theatre.

Denys Phillips) played a major supportive role by being present at the various commemorations and well-organised functions.

Street victory celebrations were held in almost every part of Torquay, Paignton and Brixham where children's tea parties, held in the open air, were the order of the day. In his official announcement of the victory speech at the Torquay Town Hall, the Mayor closed his moving speech with 'Let us then, today, clap our hands with joy, dance, sing and above all thank the Lord who has given us the victory.'

There were no less joyous celebrations at Brixham when between three and four thousand people took part in al fresco dancing at Bolton Cross during the daytime and evening of V.E. Day. At midnight, a two minutes silence was observed followed by joyous cheering. Several areas of the town entertained children to V.E. Day street tea parties.

The Imperial Hotel was beautifully decorated with flags of the Allied Nations and bunting. There were special menus for all meals and, at night, there was a Victory Dinner, Ball and Cabaret. The waiters wore red, white and blue ties and rosettes, and Allied flags decorated the tables. The speeches of Winston Churchill and the King were relayed. During the ball there was a special issue of punch which, while the lights were extinguished, was brought in on a flaming trolley by Joseph, a member of staff, who was dressed in a kilt of red, white and blue, and a Scottish bonnet. Mr H. M. Chapman, the manager, then proposed the toast of 'Victory and Allied Flags'.

A street party in Princess Street, Babbacombe, celebrating VE Day, May 1945.

THE BOOK OF TORBAY

These two photos are of Brixham Youth Club's Annual Social Supper at the Town Hall in December 1946. The occasion also celebrated VE Day and VJ Day. Among the names of those included in the photograph are: Davey, Pricton, Lovell, Pocock, Pocock, Piper, Lorain, Lawrence, Twyman, Jenkins, Thomas, Trant, Doble, Tooley, Elliott, Gorman, Aster, Dickensen, Youlden, Bond, Cummins, Warner, Butler, Baker, Nomis, Bowden, Dumbleton and Ansell.

Above: *Children on Paignotn Sands watching a Punch and Judy Show c. 1945.*

Left: *Brixham Harbour and fish market.*

Below: *The view over Meadfoot Beach c. 1935.*

28 – Picture Parade

The pictures on these final pages provide a glimpse of Torbay's past, reminding us of the place as it used to be. As we move towards a new millennium it is important to look back as well as forward, if only to reflect on the lives of the people of Torbay who came before us.

Above: *The Pendennis Castle express on the line near Paignton c. 1950.*

Left: *1930s Newspaper advertisement for Bobby's café.*

Above: *William Brown, an old Torquay boatman, prepares his lunch on a driftwood fire c.1890.*

Top: *One of the hundreds of elegant houses that was built in Torquay around the end of the nineteenth century. Houses such as 'Quintella', now where Quita Road stands, were the fashionable villas of the wealthy who, along with their servants, would summer at Torquay. After the Great War many of these villas, now too expensive to maintain as family homes, became hotels and guest houses.*

Above: *The view across Ellacombe from 'Quintella' in 1890.*

Right: *Williams & Cox provided ladies with the latest in fashionable hats in the 1930s.*

THE BOOK OF TORBAY

Top: *Louville Camp, Paignton in 1938. The arrival of affordable motoring gave the public a chance to sample the delights of a seaside holiday, and camps such as this, with tents, caravans or permanent huts, gave the place a special atmosphere. These were the forerunners of the Holiday Camp made famous by Billy Butlin and others.*

Left and below: *Contemporary advertisements encouraging holidaymakers to Paignton.*

121

Left: *A hay waggon rumbles through Cockington in the days before it became one of the areas greatest holiday attractions.*

Right: *Preston Sands in the 1890s. This whole area of coast was undeveloped at this time and would have been a truly delightful place for the Victorian child to explore.*

Left: *As the Victorians developed Torquay, so the individual villas were incorporated into small communities, while roads and other amenities were constructed. This view over Ellacombe to the quarries beyond provide a glimpse of this landscape in transition.*

Top: *Torquay's Carnival Queen being crowned in 1932.*

Above: *Brixham in the 1930s, the harbour filled with boats from the Brixham fishing fleet.*

Left: *In the 1930s it was possible to fly to Torquay via Haldon aerodrome. There were two services a day, with the return flight from Plymouth costing £2.*

THE BOOK OF TORBAY

Subscribers

Mr and Mrs J. Aggett, Torquay, Devon
Marion C. Algar, Rochester, Kent
Bryan E. Algar, Torquay, Devon
John Andrews, Torquay, Devon
Frank Annear, Torquay, Devon
Alan and Jean Ashdown, Torquay, Devon
Lorna K. Axworthy, Brixham, Devon
Geraldine Bacon, Torquay, Devon
Rachael D. Baker, Torquay, Devon
John Patrick Baker, Torquay, Devon
Keith Peter Baker, Torquay, Devon
Patricia W. V. Baker (née Pearce), Torquay, Devon
John Stuart Bannister, Torquay, Devon
Isabelle Barker (née Smardon), Brixham, Devon
David J. Barr, Galmpton, Brixham, Devon
Mr and Mrs H. G. Bartlett, Brixham, Devon
Audrey M. Bartlett, Brixham, Devon
Mr and Mrs W. Beaumont, Paignton, Devon
Irene W. Bell, Brixham, Devon
John and Anne Bennett, Torquay, Devon
Rodney Binmore, Torquay, Devon
Keith A. Blackmore, Torquay, Devon
Charles Blake F.R.I.B.A., Torquay, Devon
Eric G. and Heather C. Blatchford, Barton,
    Torquay, Devon
Trevor and Diana Bond, Brixham, Devon
Anne F. Bourdeaux, Torquay, Devon
Daisy E. Bowden (née Rogers), formerly of
    Brixham, Devon
Christopher Boyce, Brixham, Devon
Alan and Mavis Braund, Torquay, Devon
Marina Bray, Brixham, Devon
R. G. Braybrooke M.B.E., Torquay, Devon
Kath Brewer, Barton, Torquay, Devon
Barbara Brimicombe, Torquay, Devon
Denis and Lynette Brown, Torquay, Devon
W. Brown, Barton, Torquay, Devon
Mrs Barbara E. Browning, Babbacombe, Torquay,
    Devon
Stanley V. Browse, Paignton, Devon
Mrs Frances M. Brunt (née Pearse), Paignton,
    Devon
Heather M. Buckpitt, Torquay, Devon
Viv Bulley, Torquay, Devon
Emma J. Bullock, Torquay, Devon
Sarah L. Bullock, Torquay, Devon
Brian G. Burnell, Brixham, Devon
Joan Gilbert Burnell, Brixham, Devon

K. J. Burrow, Bucks Cross, Bideford, Devon
Mr and Mrs Glyn Burton, Torquay, Devon
John and Anne Carr (née Fairclough),
    Wadebridge, Cornwall
Rosemary Carter (née Wyatt), Ellacombe,
    Torquay, Devon
Mrs Christine Cavanna, Torquay, Devon
Dawn and Vaughan Charlton, Brixham, Devon
David Vaughan Charlton, Brixham, Devon
Ralph C. Chidgey, Torquay, Devon
John W. Christer, Paignton, Devon
John F. Churchill, Burnham-on-Crouch
John B. Clark, St Marychurch, Devon
Audrey F. Collier, Galmpton, Brixham, Devon
Revd Priscilla G. H. Cooke, Torquay, Devon
Margaret and Richard Cord, Torquay, Devon
J. and K. Cox, Churston, Brixham, Devon
Derek Cox, Torquay, Devon
Sharron J. Cox, Torquay, Devon
Mrs J. Crimp, Paignton, Devon
Mr Jansen Crouch, Torquay, Devon
Mrs I. M. Davey, Paignton, Devon
Mrs B. A. Davies, Brixham, Devon
Muriel Davis, Brixham, Torbay, Devon
Margaret Ann Dodd, Paignton, Devon
The Doyles, Hillhead, Brixham, Devon
Mr J. E. Drake, Torquay, Devon
Mrs Sheila M. Drake (née Battershill), Paignton,
    Devon
Patricia Duquette, Torquay, Devon
Kenneth J. Dustan, Torquay, Devon
Eileen R. Easton, Torquay, Devon
Derek W. Eaves, Brixham, Devon
Colin and June Edwards, Preston, Paignton,
    Devon
Jonathan C. Elliott, Torquay, Devon
Mrs W. Ellis, Torquay, Devon
George W. H. Ellis, Torquay, Devon
Dr Andy Ellis, Brixham, Devon
Celia Embury (Stevens), Cullompton, Devon
Ivor R. Evans, Brixham, Devon
R. and J. Facey, Torquay, Devon
Tony and Eileen Fairclough (née Blatchford), for-
    merly of Torquay, Devon
Robert Finch, Paignton, Devon
Linda and Phil Findlay,
Vince Flower, Torquay, Devon
Jonathan Ford, Paignton, Devon

THE BOOK OF TORBAY

Lynn and Robert Foster, Torquay, Devon
Kenneth J. Foster, Paignton, Devon
T. J. and C. C. Foster, Brixham, Devon
A. B. Geddes, Paignton, Devon
Mr and Mrs J. Gibbes, Torquay, Devon
Jessie K. Gibbons, Torquay, Devon
Alan C. G. Gibbs, Fulbourn, Cambridge
Ronald C. N. Gibbs, Torquay, Devon
Adrian P. Gibbs, Paignton, Devon
Peter N. H. Gibbs, Paignton, Devon
Jean M. Gill,
Mary and Jim Gill, Torquay, Devon 1999
John A. Goree, Paignton, Devon
Gladys Green, Torquay, Devon
Russell Green, Torquay, Devon
Mrs Betty Short Guilfoyle, Shiphay, Torquay, Devon
Moonyeene D. J. Gwinnell, Brixham, Devon
Trevor J. Haddleton, Teignmouth, Devon
Mr R. Hailey, Plymouth, Devon
Mavis and Norman Hannaford, Taunton, Somerset
Judith A. Hardcastle, Paignton, Devon
Roger Harris, Torquay, Devon
Sophie Harris, Galmpton, Brixham, Devon
Mr David A. Harris, Torquay, Devon
Brian and Rosemary Harris, Torquay, Devon
Mr B. D. Harris, Brixham, Devon
Mr George Harris, Brixham, Devon
Mrs T. Harris, Churston, Brixham, Devon
Beatrice R. Harris, Torquay, Devon
Vivien I. Harris, Ellacombe, Torquay, Devon
Robert D. Harrison, Brixham, Devon
Brian Hart, Brixham, Devon
David Hassell, Axbridge, Somerset
Jeremy and Gill Hassell, Edgbaston, Birmingham
Jonathan and Susan Hassell, Torquay, Devon
Pat and Bob Hawes, Torquay, Devon
Barbara L. Hawke, Torquay, Devon
Jane Hewitt, Manaton, Devon
Lionel and Amy Hill, Brixham, Devon
Wendy Hillgrove, Torquay, Devon
Ian and Jane Holloway, Torquay, Devon
Stephen Hooper, Paignton, Devon
Mr Ryan W. Hooper, Torquay, Devon
Sydney W. Hopkins, Torquay, Devon
Mrs Ann Horner, Torquay, Devon
Angela M. Howard, Paignton, Devon
Dorothy Howe, Brixham, Devon
Lorraine Howes, Torquay, Devon
Mr Peter Feltham Hunt, Brixham, Devon
Doreen James, Brixham, Devon
Peter and Sandra Jeavons, Brixham, Devon
Peter C. Jenkins, Paignton, Devon
Emily S. M. Johns, Torquay, Devon

Christine and William Johns, Paignton, Devon
Sandra and David Johnson, Chelston, Torquay
Janet A. G. Jones, St Marychurch, Torquay, Devon
Jeanette Jones, Torquay, Devon
Eileen Kelly, Torquay, Devon
Elizabeth and Michael Kenworthy-Browne, Oxford
Mrs M. L. A. Khan, London NW2
Eric W. Kinch, Torquay, Devon
Anne Knight, Cheltenham, Glos.
Justina Knight (née Harris), Paignton, Devon
A. Knowles, Brixham, Devon
Margaret E. Lake, Brixham, Devon
Terry Leaman, Torquay, Devon
Ron Levett, Torquay, Devon
Maureen Lidster (née Marchant), Torquay, Devon
George H. Lidstone, Torquay, Devon
Dawn M. Lockyer, Galmpton, Brixham, Devon
Mildred Eric Long, Torquay, Devon
Rona Lovegrove, Brixham, Devon
Michael F. Low, Torquay, Devon
Raymond C. Luckhurst, Brixham, Devon
David and Chris Margetts, Canada
Rob and Chris Margetts, Torquay, Devon
Paul Martin, Torquay, Devon
Maisie and Richard Matthews, Paignton, Devon
Reginald J. Maunder, Paignton, Devon
Elizabeth A. Maynard, Barton, Torquay, Devon
Mrs S. and Mr K. McIver, Torquay, Devon
Mr K. and Mrs H. Mears, Livermead, Torquay, Devon
Reginald J. Merrifield, Torquay, Devon
Christopher Milford, Torquay, Devon
Keith Miller, Torquay, Devon
Jean Mills, Brixham, Devon
Sandra A. Mills, Torquay, Devon
John F. Milsom, Torquay, Devon
Laurence H. Mitchell, Torquay, Devon
Dennis E. J. Mooney, Torquay, Devon
Alan G. Mooney, Torquay, Devon
Dr J. H. S. Morgan, Brixham, Devon
Ann P. Morris, Torquay, Devon
Jack Morris, Brixham, Devon
Mr J. P. and Mrs M. A. Moss, Brixham, Devon
Tony Moss, Paignton, Devon
Brian Muscroft, Brixham, Devon
Malin J. Neale, Torquay, Devon
Ray and Janet Nickells, Torquay, Devon
Peter J. Northcott, Torquay, Devon
Malcolm Northcott, Perth, Australia
Mrs M. Nunn, Cheriton Fitzpaine, Crediton, Devon
Shane A. and Deborah Anne Ogborne, Brixham, Devon

THE BOOK OF TORBAY

Beryl J. Palmer, Torquay, Devon
Mrs Jean M. Park, Paignton, Devon
Alex, Julie, Jennifer and Laura Parkes, Torquay, Devon
Margaret and Denis Parkin and Family, Paignton, Devon
Bill and Jean Passmore, Adelaide, Australia
Richard Patrick, Torquay, Devon
Susan M. Payne, Torquay, Devon
John V. Pearce, Torquay, Devon
Bernard E. Pearce, Brixham, Devon
Reginald A. L. Pearse, Paignton, Devon
Mr Vic Pells, Torquay, Devon
Derek C Pering, Torquay, Devon
Philip Perrett, Brixham, Devon
John Perrett, Torquay, Devon
Jeff Perry, Torquay, Devon
Ivor G. Pitman, Brixham, Devon
Mark Pool, Torquay, Devon
Mr and Mrs T. Pool, Ilsington
John H. Pope, Brixham, Devon
Margaret Pottinger, Torquay, Devon
R. J. Proctor, Brixham, Devon
Paula C. Radford, Paignton, Devon
Ian Richards, Brixham, Devon
Mr Arthur C. B. Rider, Torquay, Devon
Harold A. Rider, Torquay, Devon
Richard W. Rider, Torquay, Devon
Stephen C. Rider, Torquay, Devon
Ruth Rivett, Brixham, Devon
Chris and Linda Roach, Paignton, Devon
Bill and Joy Roberts, Torquay, Devon
Dulcie K. Roe, Brixham, Devon
Trevor Rogers, Brixham, Devon
Ethel Shepherd (born 1900), Stoke Gabriel, Paignton, Devon
A. F. Sherrell, Paignton, Devon
Mrs C. W. Simcock, Shiphay, Torquay, Devon
David J. Simmons, Torquay, Devon
Brenda Sims, Brixham, Devon
Mrs J. Sloman, Brixham, Devon
Michael J. and Paula Smith, Brixham, Devon
Gerald and Anna Snuggs, Brixham, Devon
Mrs R. G. Soper, Brixham, Devon
Philip A. Spray, Livermead, Torquay, Devon
Lola St John-Clifford, Torquay, Devon
Les Staples, Torquay, Devon
Mr G. W. Stephens, Paignton, Devon
Miss V. M. Stephens, Paignton, Devon
Mrs A. E. Stevens, Brixham, Devon
Pamela Stone (née Marchant), Cheltenham
Mr G. E. Taft, Paignton, Devon

Derek and Cecilia Tanner, Shiphay, Torquay, Devon
Mr D. Tarr, Torquay, Devon
Brian M. Taylor, Churston Village, Brixham, Devon
R. J. and J. A. Taylor, Torquay, Devon
David J. Taylor, Torquay, Devon
Dr Bryan Taylor O.B.E., Brixham, Devon
Pamela J. S. Teale, Galmpton, Brixham, Devon
Oliver Thomas, Torquay, Devon
Gary and Julie Thompson, Torquay, Devon
David E. Thomson, Brixham, Devon
Torquay Central Library, Torquay, Devon
Torquay Natural History Society, Torquay, Devon
Torre Abbey Historic House and Gallery, Torquay, Devon
Mr P. G. Tozer, Torquay, Devon
The Revd Prebendary B. R. Tubbs, Paignton, Devon
Ronald P. Tucker,
Mr Robert J. Tucker, Paignton, Devon
Jean Turnbull (Stevens), Paignton, Devon
David Turner, Brixham, Devon
Charles F. Turner, Torquay, Devon
Arthur H. Vowden, Torquay, Devon
John B. Vowden, Torquay, Devon
Philip Wade, Torquay, Devon
Mr and Mrs D. A. Wallis, Brixham, Devon
Dora E. Warren (née Langdon), Ellacombe, Torquay, Devon
Dr David G. Watters, Brixham, Devon
Reg Webster, Paignton, Devon
Dorothy M. West, Paignton, Devon
Dennis A. West, Paignton, Devon
Ian W. Western, Torquay, Devon
J. Philip Westwell, Torquay, Devon
E. E. M. Wheeler, Torquay, Devon
Mrs Edna L. White, St Marychurch, Torquay, Devon
Olive Wilcock, Brixham, Devon
Phyllis Williams, Paignton, Devon
Mrs J. Williams, Paignton, Devon
Leslie W. G. Williams, Torquay, Devon
Andrea J. Williams, Torquay, Devon
Ken Windeatt, Ellacombe, Torquay, Devon
Carol A. Windsor, Hill Head, Brixham, Devon
Woodlands Guest House, Brixham, Devon
Graham Wright, Brixham, Devon
Sandra Joyce Wright, Brixham, Devon
W. J. G. Wright, Galmpton, Brixham, Devon
Leonard Wyatt, Ellacombe, Torquay, Devon